THE ABRIDGED
HEBREW
BIBLE

Other books by Samuel Bavli

Biblical commentary

The Light of the Torah

Fiction for adults

The Twelfth Stone

Fiction for middle-grade readers

The Secret of the Sphinx

PRAISE FOR *THE LIGHT OF THE TORAH*

"I have very much enjoyed reading Dr. Shmuel Bavli's essays on the *parshiyot ha-shavua*. Written very clearly and drawing upon a wide range of sources—from Talmudic through modern times—Dr. Bavli has brought new insights to paths well-trodden, providing creative interpretations for many biblical narratives and laws. I have learned a lot from his thoughtful and most interesting perspectives. All will benefit from these reflections, beginners and scholars alike."

—**Rabbi Dr. Jacob J. Schacter**
*University Professor of Jewish History and Jewish Thought,
Yeshiva University, New York, NY*

"Dr. Samuel Bavli is a lover of Torah. Throughout a life of devotion to medicine as an esteemed endocrinologist, he nurtured his passion for scripture by regular study and by writing well-researched essays on the weekly portion. He has now made these available to the public, to the delight, enrichment and inspiration of us all."

—**Rabbi Haskel Lookstein**
Rabbi Emeritus of Congregation Kehilath Jeshurun, New York, NY

"I am pleased to offer high praise of Dr. Samuel Bavli's wonderfully engaging and deeply insightful work, *The Light of the Torah*. It reflects the remarkable breadth of knowledge of my friend and colleague, in both the Torah and our contemporary reality. Dr. Bavli has truly provided us with insight and wisdom that is so valuable for the thinking Jew of today. Kol Hakavod!"

—**Rabbi Kenneth Hain**
Rabbi, Congregation Beth Sholom, Lawrence, NY

SAMUEL BAVLI

THE ABRIDGED HEBREW BIBLE

A LONG STORY MADE SHORT

TAMBORA BOOKS

Copyright © 2024 by Samuel Bavli. All rights reserved.

No part of this book may be used or reproduced in any manner whatsoever without written permission, except in the case of brief quotations embodied in critical articles or reviews.

Published by Tambora Books.

ISBN 978-1-7376743-6-8

To my father, the Hebrew poet Hillel Bavli.

And with a song of prayer
I will again be joined to the bosom of existence.

—From A FUGITIVE OF LIFE

A poem by Hillel Bavli (1961)

Translation by Samuel Bavli

CONTENTS

Biblical Chronology xi

Kings of Israel and Judea xiii

Introduction xv

THE TORAH

    I. GENESIS (*Bereshit*) 3

    II. EXODUS (*Shemot*) 21

    III. LEVITICUS (*Vayikra*) 37

    IV. NUMBERS (*Bamidbar*) 44

    V. DEUTERONOMY (*Devarim*) 59

THE PROPHETS

Early Prophets:

    JOSHUA 73

    JUDGES 81

    1 SAMUEL 91

    2 SAMUEL 103

    1 KINGS 111

    2 KINGS 121

Late Prophets:

    ISAIAH 134

    JEREMIAH 144

EZEKIEL 155

The Twelve Prophets:

HOSEA 161

JOEL 162

AMOS 163

OBADIAH 164

JONAH 164

MICAH 165

NAHUM 166

HABAKKUK 166

ZEPHANIAH 167

HAGGAI 167

ZECHARIAH 168

MALACHI 170

THE WRITINGS

PSALMS (*Tehillim*) 173

PROVERBS (*Mishlei*) 183

JOB 187

The Five Megillot:

THE SONG OF SONGS 189

RUTH 189

LAMENTATIONS (*Eicha*) 190

ECCLESIASTES (*Kohelet*) 190

ESTHER... 192

DANIEL 196

EZRA 200

NEHEMIAH.. 202

CHRONICLES 205

Acknowledgements 207

About the Author................................... 209

Index of Names and Places 211

BIBLICAL CHRONOLOGY

Years BCE	Event
?	Creation. Adam and Eve.
?	Noah. The Flood.
?	The Patriarchs: Abraham, Isaac, & Jacob.
?	Joseph is brought to Egypt as a slave.
c. 1290 (?)	The birth of Moses.
c. 1210 (?)	The Exodus from Egypt.
c. 1170 (?)	The Israelites enter Canaan.
c. 1008	David becomes king of Israel.
c. 968	Solomon becomes king of Israel.
c. 965	King Solomon begins building the Temple in Jerusalem.
c. 925	The ten northern tribes secede during the reign of Rehoboam. Israel is divided into two kingdoms—Israel and Judea. Rehoboam continues as king of Judea only (comprising the tribes of Judah and Benjamin), while Jeroboam I reigns in Israel.
760	The great earthquake in Jerusalem. King Uzziahu becomes a leper. According to tradition, it is said that Isaiah begins to prophesy at this time.
745–727	Reign of King Tiglath-Pileser III of Assyria.
727–722	Reign of King Shalmaneser V of Assyria.
722–705	Reign of King Sargon II of Assyria.
722	King Sargon II of Assyria conquers the ten tribes of Israel (the northern kingdom) and sends them all into exile.
715–686	Reign of King Hezekiah of Judea.
705–681	Reign of King Sennacherib of Assyria.
701	Sennacherib besieges Jerusalem but fails to conquer it.
c. 640–609	Reign of King Josiah of Judea. Jeremiah begins to prophesy in the 13th year of Josiah's reign.
597	Nebuchadnezzar II, king of Babylonia, exiles King Jehoiachin (Jechoniah) of Judea to Babylonia, along with many of the leading citizens of Jerusalem.

593	Ezekiel begins to prophesy in Babylonia.
586	Nebuchadnezzar II sacks Jerusalem, burns the Temple to the ground, and exiles many of the remaining inhabitants of Judea to Babylonia.
559–530	Reign of Cyrus II as king of Persia. He founds the Persian Empire in 550 BCE.
539	Cyrus II conquers Babylonia.
538	Cyrus II issues a proclamation permitting the Jews (i.e. the people of Judea now living in exile in Babylonia) to return to their land and rebuild the Temple in Jerusalem. (The book of Ezra dates this proclamation to the first year of Cyrus. Since Ezra lived in Babylonia, the dating probably refers to Cyrus's first year of ruling over Babylonia, which he conquered in 539 BCE.)
522–486	Reign of Darius I (Darius the Great) of Persia.
516	The Second Temple is completed.
486–465	Reign of Xerxes I (Ahasuerus) of Persia. The story of the book of Esther begins in the 3rd year of his reign.
465–424	Reign of Artaxerxes I of Persia. He sends Ezra the Scribe to Jerusalem in the seventh year of his reign.
c. 445	Nehemiah arrives in Jerusalem.

KINGS OF ISRAEL AND JUDEA

ALL DATES ARE BCE, AND ALL DATES ARE APPROXIMATIONS (PROBABLY WITHIN 2 YEARS).
DATES MENTIONED IN THE BOOK OF KINGS SOMETIMES INCLUDE A KING'S COREGENCY.

SAUL (C.1027-1008)
DAVID (C.1008-968)
SOLOMON (C.968-928)

THE TEN NORTHERN TRIBES SECEDE, AND THE KINGDOM IS DIVIDED (925)

KINGDOM OF ISRAEL	KINGDOM OF JUDEA
JEROBOAM (925-907)	REHOBOAM (C.928-911)
	ABIJAH (ABIJAM) (911-909)
NADAB (907-906)	ASA (909-868)
BAASHA (906-883)
ELAH (883-882)
ZIMRI (882)
OMRI (882-871)
AHAB (870-851)	JEHOSHAPHAT (867-851)
AHAZIAH (851-850)	JEHORAM (851-843)
JEHORAM (850-842)	AHAZIAH (843-842)
JEHU (842-814)	QUEEN ATALIA (841-835)
	JOASH (835-796)
JEHOAHAZ (814-800)
JOASH (800-785)	AMAZIAH (796-767)
JEROBOAM II (785-750)	UZZIAHU (790-767)?COREGENT
	UZZIAHU (767-738)SOLE RULER
ZECHARIAH (750)	JOTHAM (751-738) COREGENT
SHALLUM (750)
MENAHEM (750-740)
PEKAHIAH (740-738)
PEKAH (738-730)	JOTHAM (738-732)SOLE RULER
HOSHEA (730-722)	AHAZ (735-732)?COREGENT
	AHAZ (732-716) SOLE RULER
	HEZEKIAH (728-715)?COREGENT
	HEZEKIAH (715-686) SOLE RULER
EXILE OF ISRAEL	MANASSEH (697-686)?COREGENT
722	MANASSEH (686-642)SOLE RULER
	AMON (642-640)
	JOSIAH (640-609)
	JEHOAHAZ (609)
	JEHOIAKIM (609-598)
	JEHOIACHIN (598-597)
	ZEDEKIAH (597-586)

EXILE OF JUDEA
586

INTRODUCTION

The Hebrew Bible is the central holy book of Judaism. It is the basis upon which the Jewish religion is built, but its influence extends far beyond the Jewish people. The Hebrew Bible is also part of the Christian canon, and moreover, its principles provide the foundation upon which the ethical code of Western civilization is built.

However, despite the importance of the Hebrew Bible, only a small minority of people have read it in its entirety. And even most people who consider the Bible to be authoritative and of divine origin nevertheless are familiar with only a small portion of its content. Many are deterred by the sheer size of the book, and others by the unfamiliar phrasing even in English translation. My goal in writing this book is to overcome those obstacles and to make the Hebrew Bible more accessible to people. Working from the original Hebrew text, I have endeavored to summarize the Hebrew Bible in a concise manner, concentrating on the essence of the text in language that is easy to understand but at the same time conveying both the plain meaning and the flavor of the Bible. All translations of the Biblical text are my own. And significantly, I have avoided interpretation or comments except in the occasional instances where otherwise the text as written would be misunderstood or might not be understood at all.

The Abridged Hebrew Bible is a succinct summary of the entire Hebrew Bible—the *Tanakh* as it is called in Hebrew. The book is intended for all people who have an interest in the Bible: both for people who have no knowledge of *Tanakh* and want to learn what is in it, and for those who have learned the Bible in the past and want to refresh their memory with a quick review.

The Hebrew Bible consists of three parts: the Torah, the Prophets, and the Writings. The first of the three parts is the Torah, which means "the Teaching." The Torah contains many laws, but its teachings go far beyond a mere presentation of the laws by which we are to live. Significantly, the Torah endeavors to give us a realization of both God's awesome power and also His concern and love for His creations. We see how He interacts with mankind and how He guides us to live righteously and to strive for holiness.

The Torah is written in the form of a history, beginning with God's creation of the world. Crucial events of early human history are presented, culminating in the origins of the Jewish people. The narrative continues with the story of the Patriarchs of Israel in the Holy Land, and God's promise to the Patriarchs to give that land to them and their progeny as their eternal inheritance. Thus, the strong, unbreakable bond of the Jewish people with the land of Israel was established. But soon, circumstances forced the clan of Israel to migrate to the land of Egypt, where they were enslaved. After several generations, God sent the great prophet Moses to deliver the Israelites from slavery and to bring them to Mount Sinai where they experienced a divine revelation and became a nation—the nation of Israel.

However, after generations of slavery in Egypt, a land that worshipped multiple deities, the people of Israel had to rid themselves of the slave mentality and of the pagan inclinations that were ingrained in their thinking. They were an unruly and a rebellious people composed of twelve contentious, squabbling tribes; and Moses struggled in his effort to guide his embryonic nation to follow the path that God had set for them. It would take many years to mold them into the sort of people that God had intended for them to become.

Israel was not to be just another nation. In those days, some of the neighboring nations practiced ritual prostitution, child sacrifice, and other acts of immorality and barbarism as part of their religion; and idolatry, injustice, and immorality were prevalent throughout the world. In contrast, Israel was to be a nation under God, a nation ruled by justice, living according to a set of laws and ethical principles that God would give them. And Israel was to be the vehicle through which the principles of justice and morality were eventually to be transmitted to the world. At Mount Sinai, God gave His nation the first ten of His laws, known as the Decalogue or the "Ten Commandments." And many additional laws were given during forty years traveling through the desert in preparation for Israel's entry into the Promised Land where their patriarchs had lived before the Egyptian exile. The Torah records those laws in the course of its historical narrative, and thus we are able to understand the context in which they were given.

The Torah continues its narrative of Moses's leadership through the contentious years in the desert and concludes with the death of Moses just as his nation is on the verge of entering into the Promised Land—the land of their ancestors, the land of their destiny.

The second part of the Hebrew Bible, "The Prophets," is divided into the "Early Prophets" and the "Late Prophets." The books of the Early Prophets continue the history of Israel after their entry into the Promised Land. At first, the nation was led by prophets such as Joshua, Deborah, and Samuel, or by divinely inspired leaders known as "Judges" such as Ehud, Gideon, and Samson. Later, the people asked to be ruled by a king, like all other nations, and God had the prophet Samuel anoint a king—first King Saul and later King David. But the king of Israel was not to be an absolute monarch like the kings of other nations: he was to rule with justice, in accordance with the laws of the Torah. And, as a check on the king's power, God appointed prophets such as Nathan, Elijah, Isaiah, and Jeremiah, to guide the kings and to reprimand them when they strayed from the path of justice and righteousness.

In approximately 925 BCE, the ten northern tribes of Israel seceded. The tribes of Judah and Benjamin—now called the Kingdom of Judea—remained faithful to the dynasty of King David, with the capital in Jerusalem, and the kings of Judea for the most part continued to rule justly. By contrast, the northern kingdom of the ten tribes—now called the Kingdom of Israel—was ruled from its capital in Samaria by a series of unjust and often tyrannical kings who promoted the worship of foreign gods. Assyria conquered the northern kingdom and exiled its people in 722 BCE.

In the southern kingdom, Judea, morality and honesty gradually declined, and the people were sorely tempted with the worship of Baal and other foreign deities, even in times when the king was devoted to God's laws. But the last four kings of Judea were sinful, unlike most of their predecessors. Babylonia conquered Judea and exiled its people to Babylonia in 586 BCE.

The books of the Late Prophets—Isaiah, Jeremiah, Ezekiel, and the twelve shorter prophetic books—contain the prophecies of those prophets, with only occasional chapters of historical narrative. Some prophecies give guidance to the people of their generation or admonish them for their shortcomings or their sins. Other prophecies are meant to strengthen and elevate the spirit of the nation; and still others are prophecies of events that will happen, either in a matter of a few years, or in the distant future.

The third part of the Hebrew Bible, "The Writings," comprises books written under divine inspiration although at a lower level of divine guidance than the prophetic books contained in the second part of the Bible. The Writings begin with Psalms, which is a book of religious poetry filled with words of devotion and prayer to God, meant to uplift the soul and bring us closer to the Lord. After Psalms, the Writings continue with books of philosophy, ethics, and wisdom such as Proverbs, Job, and Ecclesiastes, which serve to round out our thinking about many basic issues pertaining to the purpose of our lives, our relationship with God and with other people, and how to live a life of holiness. And there are books of historical narrative, which highlight major periods in the history of the people of Israel. The book of Ruth, set in the period of the Judges, presents the unfolding of the events that led to fruition of God's plan to have Israel ruled by kings descended from Judah, and from Ruth, a Moabite convert to Judaism. The books of Esther, Daniel, Ezra, Nehemiah, and Chronicles continue the history of Israel after its exile from its land, describing the Israelites' tribulations and their eventual return to the Promised Land.

In reading the Hebrew Bible, we can see the hand of God working through history, guiding the people of Israel, and indeed all of mankind. Sometimes God's guidance is delivered through prophecy, and on rare occasions God intervenes directly in the course of history through miracles. We see God's hand in the historical narrative told by the Torah and the later historical books, and we see it in the prophecies of the Late Prophets. Often, the path is winding, and at times it goes far off course, because God has given each of us free will to choose our actions. Evil frequently is disguised and tempts us with appealing promises of a bright future. Our leaders, and great swaths of humanity, may be misled and only much later recognize their error. Mankind in general, and the nation of Israel in particular, have many times gone astray, but eventually they return, and in the aggregate, mankind eventually returns to follow the path that God ordained.

THE TORAH

I. THE BOOK OF GENESIS (*Bereshit*)

In the beginning, God created the heaven and the earth, and darkness enveloped the world. God said, "Let there be light!" And there was light. Again, God spoke; and each day, His words called more things into being: heaven and earth, stars and planets, plants and animals, and finally humans. Then, after six days, God's work was complete, and He stopped creating. He blessed the seventh day and sanctified it. (Genesis, Chapter 1, & 2:1–3)

The creation of Adam and Eve, the first humans. God created humans in His image, and He imbued them with His spirit. Male and female He created them; He placed them in the Garden of Eden; and He blessed them, telling them to be fruitful and multiply and rule over the earth. But the snake tempted Eve to eat of the Tree of Knowledge, which God had forbidden. First Eve ate the fruit. She offered it to Adam, and he ate it also. As punishment for their disobedience, God banished Adam and Eve from the garden. (1:27–28, & 2:4 – 3:24)

Cain and Abel: the first murder. Out of jealousy, Cain, the son of Adam, killed his brother Abel. Cain repented and went into exile; but he feared that his reputation would precede him, and people would seek to kill him. Therefore, the Lord gave Cain a mark, as a sign that he should not be killed. (Chapter 4)

The corruption of mankind. After the death of Abel, Adam and Eve had another son, and they named him Seth (*Shet*), followed by other sons and daughters. Adam died at the age of 930 years, and humans continued to proliferate. In the eight generations following Adam, most notable were Enoch, who walked with God, and God took him at the age of 365 years; and Enoch's son Methuselah, who lived 969 years. After Adam, successive generations turned to wickedness; and in the tenth generation, man's wickedness reached its zenith. God decided to wipe out all life on the face of the earth: both man and beast, and also birds. But one man was worthy of being saved. His name was Noah. (4:25 – 6:8)

The Great Flood. Noah was a righteous man. God told Noah of His plan to bring a flood to annihilate all life on earth; and He commanded Noah to build a huge ark, to save himself, his family, and representatives of each type of animal, both male and female. Rain fell for forty days and forty nights, and the ground water rose, so that even the mountains were covered. After about a year, the ark came to rest on Mount Ararat. Twice, Noah sent out a dove; and when the dove didn't return after the second time, Noah knew that water no longer covered the earth. Upon leaving the ark, Noah built an altar and brought a burnt offering to the Lord. (6:9 – 8:22)

God's covenant with Noah. God blessed Noah and his children. For the first time, God now permitted humans to eat meat; and he gave Noah laws by which humankind were to live, including the prohibition of murder. God vowed to Noah that He will never again bring a flood to annihilate all life on earth; and He said to Noah that the rainbow would be a sign of the covenant and a reminder to future generations of God's vow. (9:1–17)

Noah's drunkenness. After emerging from the ark, Noah planted a vineyard. He drank wine and became intoxicated. While Noah lay in his tent in a drunken stupor, his son Ham entered and saw his father naked. Ham told his two brothers Shem and Japheth. Shem and Japheth entered the tent with their faces respectfully averted, and covered their father's nakedness. When Noah awoke and realized what had been done to him, he cursed Canaan, the son of Ham. (9:18–29)

Noah's progeny. Noah's sons—Shem, Ham, and Japheth—each had sons born to them after the flood, and from them came all the nations of world. Ham's grandson Nimrod was the first conqueror. (Chapter 10)

The division and dispersion of humankind. The people of Shinar sought to challenge God. They resolved to build a great city—Babylon (*Bavel*)—with a tower whose peak would reach into the heavens. God confused their speech, so they could no longer understand each other. They stopped building the city, and God dispersed them throughout the land. (11:1–9)

The descendants of Shem. In the ninth generation from Shem, his descendant was Terah. Terah lived in the city of Ur with his two oldest sons, Abram and Nahor. Terah's third son died young, leaving a son named Lot. Abram took a wife named Sarai, but she was barren. Terah left Ur, taking with him Abram and Sarai, and Lot his grandson. When they came to the city of Haran, they settled there. And Terah died in Haran. (11:10–32)

The Promised Land. The Lord spoke to Abram and told him to leave his father's home and go to the land that the Lord will show him. Abram went, and Lot went with him. God led Abram to the land of Canaan, and He promised to give that land to Abram's descendants. (12:1–9)

Abram's descent into Egypt. There was a famine in the land,

and Abram went to Egypt to escape the famine. Fearing that the Egyptians—seeing his wife Sarai's beauty—would kill him and take his wife, Abram told Sarai to say she was his sister. And indeed, Pharaoh's officials took Sarai for Pharaoh's harem. The Lord afflicted Pharaoh and his household with illness; and when Pharaoh discovered that Sarai was Abram's wife, he banished both of them from Egypt. Abram and Sarai returned to Canaan with their belongings. (12:1–20)

Abram and Lot. After leaving Egypt, Abram and Sarai lived in the Negev, and Lot came with them. But both Abram and Lot had many sheep and cattle; and there was insufficient grazing land for both their herds. Therefore they separated, and Lot relocated to the environs of the evil city of Sodom. After Lot's departure, God told Abram to walk through the land, to take possession of it. (Chapter 13)

The war of Sodom against Elam. The king of Sodom, with three allied kings, went to war against the king of Elam. The Elamites and their allies conquered Sodom, and Abram's nephew Lot was taken captive. Abram quickly assembled an army and pursued the Elamites. He defeated the Elamites and rescued Lot. With the defeat of the Elamites, the king of Sodom also regained his freedom, and he offered to reward Abram. But Abram refused to accept as much as a shoelace from the evil king of Sodom. (Chapter 14)

God's covenant with Abram. The Lord made a covenant with Abram, assuring him that he will have children and that they will inherit the land. But, God said, Abram's descendants will first be enslaved in a foreign land and will be oppressed there. God, however, will punish the oppressors, and the fourth generation will return to inherit the land of Canaan, from the River of Egypt to the Euphrates River. (Chapter 15)

Sarai, Hagar, and Ishmael. Sarai, who was still childless, gave her Egyptian slave-woman Hagar to Abram as a concubine, for him to have a child by her, and the child would be considered Sarai's offspring. But when Hagar got pregnant, Sarai oppressed her, and Hagar fled into the desert. An angel came to Hagar and told her to return to Sarai, assuring her that her son will be a man of great prowess. Hagar gave birth to a son, and his name was Ishmael— "God will listen." Abram was then eighty years old. (Chapter 16)

Abram and Sarai's new names. When Abram was ninety-nine years old, God appeared to Abram and reaffirmed His covenant, saying He will give Abram's future descendants the entire land of Canaan as an eternal inheritance. He commanded Abram that thenceforth all male children were to be circumcised at the age of eight days. And, God said, Abram's name was now to be Abraham, and Sarai was now to be called Sarah. Finally, God told Abraham that his wife Sarah will have a son. Abraham laughed, because he was ninety-nine and Sarah was ninety years of age. But God said that Sarah will indeed have a son, and—although Ishmael will also be a great man and the father of a nation—it will be Sarah's son who will inherit God's covenant. Abraham then carried out God's command, circumcising himself and the members of his household. Abraham was ninety-nine years old, and Ishmael was thirteen years old when they were circumcised. (Chapter 17)

The three angels. Three angels came to Abraham's tent, disguised as men. The angels told Abraham that within the year, Sarah will have a son. Sarah overheard, and she laughed to herself, because she was too old to bear children. But God said to Abraham, "Is there anything that is beyond the Lord?" (18:1–15)

The iniquity of Sodom. God told Abraham that the sinfulness of Sodom had become too great to tolerate. As the angels departed Abraham's tent on their way to Sodom, Abraham argued with God to spare the city, saying it would be unjust to kill the innocent with the guilty. And God agreed that if there were ten righteous people in Sodom, He would spare the city. (18:16–33)

The destruction of Sodom. Two of the angels arrived in Sodom and informed Lot that they were there to destroy the city, but Lot hesitated to leave. The angels took Lot, his wife, and his two daughters by their hands and led them out of the city, telling them that they must not look back to see the city's destruction. But, as God rained fire and brimstone on the cities of Sodom and Gomorrah and the neighboring cities, Lot's wife looked back, and she was turned into a pillar of salt. (19:1–30)

Lot and his daughters. Lot was afraid to stay in Tso'ar, the one city in the region that was not destroyed; so he went to the mountains and lived in a cave with his daughters. The elder daughter remarked to her sister that there was no man with whom to procreate. So they gave their father wine, and each daughter lay with him on successive nights. He didn't realize what was happening, and they both became pregnant. The elder daughter's son became the father of the nation of Moab; the younger daughter's son was the father of the Ammonites. (19:31–38)

Abraham and Sarah in Gerar. Abraham and Sarah went to Gerar, in the land of the Philistines. Sarah said she was Abraham's sister, and Abimelekh, the king of Gerar took her into his harem. In a dream, God told Abimelekh that Sarah was married, and he will die unless he returns her to her husband. When Abimelekh asked Abraham why he had represented Sarah as his sister, Abraham said he had feared for his life. Also, Abraham added, Sarah was in fact his half-sister. Abimelekh promptly returned Sarah to Abraham, gave Abraham lavish presents, and told him he may settle wherever he liked best in Abimelekh's domain. (Chapter 20)

The banishment of Hagar and Ishmael. Sarah gave birth to a son, and Abraham named him Isaac—"he will laugh." As Isaac grew older, his half-brother Ishmael became a bad influence. Sarah demanded that Abraham expel the slave-woman and her son. Abraham was distressed, but God told Abraham to listen to Sarah, and Abraham banished Hagar and Ishmael. Hagar and Ishmael wandered in the desert and ran out of water. But an angel appeared to Hagar and showed her a well. Ishmael grew up, and God was with him. And his mother took for him a wife from the land of Egypt. (21:1–21)

Abraham's treaty with Abimelekh. Abimelekh saw that God was with Abraham. At Abimelekh's request, they made a treaty, which was to be binding on their sons and grandsons, and included an acknowledgement of Abraham's property rights to certain wells. (21:22–34)

The binding of Isaac. God tested Abraham by telling him to go to a certain mountain and sacrifice his son Isaac. Abraham arose early in the morning and went with Isaac to fulfill the Lord's command. On reaching the mountain, Abraham built an altar and bound Isaac on the altar; but an angel stopped Abraham at the last moment, and Abraham sacrificed a ram in place of his son. (Chapter 22)

The family burial plot: the Cave of Machpelah. Sarah died in Hebron. Abraham contracted with the local Hittite chieftain to buy the Cave of Machpelah for a burial site, for four hundred shekels of silver. (Chapter 23)

Isaac's marriage. Abraham told his trusted slave Eliezer to find a wife for Isaac. He had Eliezer take an oath not to select a wife from among the Canaanites but to go to Aram, the homeland of Abraham's family, to find a wife. Eliezer arrived at a well in the city of Abraham's family, and he prayed to God to help him find the right woman. Indeed, so it was: Rebekah, the granddaughter of Abraham's brother Nahor, happened by the well. After discussion with Rebekah's family, an agreement was reached, and Rebekah consented to go to Canaan with Eliezer. Isaac and Rebekah married, and Isaac loved her. (Chapter 24)

Abraham's last years. Abraham took another wife, named Keturah; and she bore him several sons, one of whom was Midian—the ancestor of the Midianites. Abraham gave the sons of his concubines presents and sent them eastward during his lifetime; and he left all that was his to his son Isaac. Abraham died at the age of 175 years, and his sons Isaac and Ishmael buried him in the Cave of Machpelah. After Abraham's death, God blessed Isaac. Ishmael had twelve sons, who became tribal chieftains and ranged over a wide territory. (25:1–18)

Isaac's twin sons: Jacob and Esau. After Isaac's marriage to Rebekah, Rebekah at first was childless. So Isaac prayed to the Lord, and Rebekah became pregnant. After a difficult pregnancy, she gave birth to twin sons. The elder twin was red and very hairy, and they named him Esau; then his brother emerged, holding onto Esau's heel, and he was named Jacob (*Ya'akov*—related to the

Hebrew word for "heel"). When the boys grew up, Esau became a hunter and a man of the field, while Jacob was a tent dweller. And Isaac had a special love for Esau. One day, Esau returned from the field, tired and hungry, and, having no regard for his birthright, he sold it to Jacob in exchange for some bread and lentil stew. (25:19–34)

Isaac in the land of the Philistines. There was another famine in the land, and God told Isaac not to go to Egypt but to remain in the land that God had promised to Isaac's father. So Isaac went to nearby Gerar, in the land of Abimelekh king of the Philistines; and there, Isaac became wealthy. The Philistines became jealous of Isaac, and they filled with earth all the wells that Abraham had dug. Abimelekh then banished Isaac from the city. Isaac re-dug his father's wells that the Philistines had blocked up. After further discord with Philistine shepherds, Isaac moved to Beer-Sheba. Abimelekh came to Isaac, bringing with him his aide, as well as the commander of his army; and they made a treaty with Isaac. Meanwhile, Esau married two Hittite women, and they were a source of great distress for Isaac and Rebekah. (Chapter 26)

Isaac's blessing. When Isaac was close to death, he wanted to bless each of his sons, and he intended to give the greater blessing to Esau. But Isaac's vision was failing, and Rebekah urged her son Jacob to disguise himself as Esau and trick his father into giving him the blessing intended for his brother. The ruse was successful, and Jacob got the greater blessing. Consequently, Esau hated Jacob and resolved to kill him after their father's death. When Rebekah heard of Esau's plan, she advised Jacob to flee, and go to her brother Laban in Haran until Esau's anger cools. (Chapter 27)

Jacob's dream. While on his journey to Haran, but before leaving Canaan, Jacob had a dream of a ladder reaching to the sky, and angels were going up and down the ladder. God spoke to Jacob in the dream and promised the land to him and his descendants. (Chapter 28)

Rachel and Leah. Jacob arrived in Haran and fell in love with his cousin Rachel. He wanted to marry her; but Rachel's father Laban—Jacob's uncle—tricked Jacob into marrying both Rachel and her sister Leah. And Jacob agreed to work as a shepherd for Laban. (29:1–30)

Leah's children. The Lord saw that Leah was not loved, and He opened her womb. Leah bore four sons to Jacob—Reuben, Simeon, Levi, and Judah—but Rachel was barren. Rachel gave her slave-woman Bilha to Jacob as a concubine, so that Rachel would have a child through her. Bilha bore a son named Dan, and another son named Naphtali. When Leah saw that she had stopped bearing children, she gave Jacob her slave-woman Zilpa as a concubine; and Zilpa bore Jacob two sons: Gad and Asher. Leah then bore a fifth son—Issachar—and a sixth son—Zebulun; and afterwards, she had a daughter named Dinah. (29:31 – 30:21)

Joseph's birth. God heard Rachel's prayers. She got pregnant and had a son, and she named him Joseph. After Joseph's birth, Jacob asked Laban to allow him to return to Canaan. Laban would not release him, and Jacob continued to tend his uncle's sheep; but Laban agreed to let Jacob select some of the sheep to keep as his own. (30:22–43)

Jacob's departure from Laban. After twenty years working for his uncle, Jacob became very wealthy. Jacob saw that Laban was no longer favorably disposed to him; so he took his wives, his children, his flock, and all his belongings, and he left, bound for his father's home in Canaan. After three days, Laban pursued Jacob. When he caught up to Jacob, he accused Jacob of cheating him, of abducting his daughters, and stealing his god—a small idol. And, Laban added that he had the power to harm Jacob, but God had spoken to him in a dream the previous night and warned him against threatening Jacob. Jacob got angry, saying that in the twenty years of his employment, he had never cheated Laban. Moreover, he had increased Laban's wealth tenfold; and, Jacob said, if God had not been with him, Laban would have sent Jacob off with nothing. Laban replied that Jacob's wives and children, and all of Jacob's possessions, actually belonged to Laban; but he made a pact with Jacob. Laban kissed his children and blessed them; and he and Jacob went their separate ways. (Chapter 31)

An angel wrestles with Jacob. Jacob sent messengers to his brother Esau with a message of appeasement, but the messengers reported back to Jacob that Esau was coming with 400 men. Jacob prepared for Esau's attack, and he prayed to God for protection. On the night before his encounter with Esau, an angel wrestled with Jacob until dawn, and the angel could not defeat him. The angel gave Jacob a new name: Israel—"he contends with the divine"—reassuring him that just as he had succeeded in fighting an angel, he can also fight against men and be successful. In the morning, Jacob and Esau met and made peace with each other. Jacob offered Esau many presents, but Esau declined the presents, saying he had much wealth already. Esau returned home, and Jacob settled in Canaan, in the town of Shechem, where he bought a parcel of land from the sons of Hamor the father of Shechem. (Chapters 32 & 33)

The rape of Dinah. Dinah, the daughter of Leah and Jacob, went to make acquaintance with the daughters of the land. Shechem, the son of Hamor the local prince, saw Dinah, who was very attractive. He fell in love with her, and he raped her. Shechem then asked his father to arrange a marriage for him with Dinah, and his father proposed the marriage to Jacob. Dinah's brothers were enraged, and two of her brothers—Simeon and Levi—avenged their sister's dishonor by killing Shechem and all the men of his town. Jacob greatly disapproved of their act, but the two brothers retorted that they could not allow their sister to be treated like a whore. (Chapter 34)

The death of Rachel. At God's command, Jacob went to Bethel, the place where previously he had dreamt of angels ascending and descending; and there, Jacob now built an altar. God spoke to him there, reaffirming that the land He had promised to Abraham and Isaac would belong to the descendants of Jacob; and many kings will descend from him. Soon after Jacob and his family left Bethel, Rachel went into labor, and she had a difficult delivery. As she was dying, the midwife informed her that the baby was a boy, and Rachel named him Ben-Oni—"the son of my sorrow"; but his father called him Benjamin. Jacob settled in Hebron, where his father Isaac dwelled. Isaac lived for 180 years, and his sons Esau and Jacob buried him. (Chapter 35)

Esau's descendants—the Edomites. The land was insufficient to support the livestock of both Jacob and Esau, so Esau moved with his family to Mount Se'ir. Esau was the father of the nation of

Edom; and eight kings reigned in Edom before any king reigned in Israel. (Chapter 36)

Joseph and his brothers. Jacob settled in the land of Canaan. Of his twelve sons, Jacob favored Joseph—the elder son of Rachel—over his other sons; and he gave Joseph a special coat, which made Joseph's brothers very jealous. Joseph had a dream showing that he will be lord over his brothers. He told the dream to his brothers, and they hated him even more. He dreamed a second dream, that the sun and the moon and eleven stars were bowing down to him, and he told that dream to his brothers and his father Jacob. Speaking to his sons, Jacob dismissed the dream as nonsense, but he kept the dream in mind. Joseph's brothers—the sons of Jacob's other wives—wanted to kill Joseph, but Judah talked them out of it. Instead, they sold Joseph into slavery, and they tried to convince their father that Joseph in fact had been killed by a wild animal. (Chapter 37)

Judah and Tamar. Judah had three sons. The oldest son married a woman named Tamar. But he died and left Tamar childless. Judah's second son then fulfilled his obligation to take Tamar in levirate marriage; but he died also. Judah was afraid to let his third son marry Tamar. So Tamar disguised herself as a harlot and tricked Judah into lying with her. Judah didn't have payment, and he gave her a security deposit. But later, when he sent a friend to retrieve his deposit, the harlot had disappeared. Three months passed, and Judah learned that Tamar was pregnant and was accused of adultery. But she presented the items that Judah had given her as security, in support of her assertion that she was pregnant by Judah, and that she was blameless. Judah admitted that she was righteous; and she bore twin sons: Peretz and Zerah. (Chapter 38)

Joseph in Egypt. The Ishmaelites who had bought Joseph brought him to Egypt and sold him to a high official named Potiphar. While Joseph was serving in Potiphar's household, Potiphar's wife tried to seduce him, but he refused her advances. She told her husband that Joseph had tried to seduce her, and Potiphar had Joseph sent to prison. (Chapter 39)

The king's cupbearer and baker. Pharaoh got angry with his cupbearer and his baker, and he put them both in prison—the same prison where Joseph was held. One night, Pharaoh's courtiers both had dreams, and they told their dreams to Joseph. Joseph interpreted their dreams: Pharaoh will reinstate the cupbearer and will execute the baker. And indeed, so it was. But the cupbearer, on being restored to his position, did not fulfill Joseph's request that he mention Joseph to the king. The cupbearer forgot Joseph completely. (Chapter 40)

Pharaoh's dream. Two years passed. Pharaoh dreamed of seven fat cows and seven emaciated cows; and the skinny cows ate the fat cows. Then he dreamed of seven plump grains of wheat and seven skinny ones; and the skinny grains ate the fat grains. He called on his wise men, but none could interpret the dreams. His cupbearer suddenly remembered Joseph and told Pharaoh about him. Pharaoh had Joseph released from prison and brought to him. Joseph explained that both dreams indicate there will be seven years of plenty followed by seven years of famine, and Joseph proposed a plan to store food during the years of plenty, to avert disaster during the seven lean years. Pharaoh recognized Joseph's wisdom. He appointed Joseph viceroy of Egypt and put him in charge of the food supply. (41:1–44)

Viceroy of Egypt. Joseph was thirty years old when he was appointed viceroy. Pharaoh gave him a wife—Asenath, daughter of Poti-Phera, Priest of On—and she bore Joseph two sons before the famine began. Joseph named the firstborn Manasseh, and the second son he called Ephraim. When the famine began, Joseph opened the storehouses and provided food for Egypt. And, because the famine was everywhere, people also came from neighboring lands to buy food. (41:45–57)

The famine in Canaan. Jacob heard that there was food to be bought in Egypt. He sent ten of his sons to Egypt; but Benjamin, his only remaining son by Rachel, he kept with him in Canaan. Arriving in Egypt, the brothers were brought before Joseph; and Joseph recognized them, but they did not recognize him. Joseph spoke to them through a translator and did not tell them his identity. He was testing them. He accused his brothers of being spies. The brothers denied it, and they told about their father, about their brother Benjamin, and about a brother who was missing. Joseph said he didn't believe their story. He chose one brother, Simeon, and put him in prison, saying he would release Simeon if the other brothers verify their tale by returning with their youngest brother. He sent the other brothers home with their food supply. (42:1–34)

The return of the brothers to Egypt. When the brothers got home to Canaan, they found their money returned in their sacks, and they became afraid. When their food supply ran out, Jacob asked his sons to return to Egypt to buy food. At first, Jacob wouldn't allow them to take Benjamin with them, lest something happen to him. But the famine remained severe, and the brothers wouldn't return to Egypt without Benjamin. Jacob finally gave in, and they went. They presented Benjamin to Joseph, and Joseph was very moved; nevertheless, he still did not reveal his identity. Joseph released Simeon, and the brothers left. But Joseph had his men plant his special goblet in Benjamin's saddle-bag. Joseph had his men chase the brothers and arrest them, accusing them of stealing the goblet. When the goblet was found in Benjamin's saddle-bag, Joseph pronounced the penalty: Benjamin will remain in Egypt as Joseph's slave, but the other brothers are free to return home. (42:35 – 44:17)

"I am Joseph." Judah, the spokesman for the brothers, described how attached their father was to his youngest son, and he pleaded with the viceroy not to take Benjamin. Judah offered to remain himself in Benjamin's stead. The viceroy could no longer contain himself; and, crying aloud, he revealed himself to his brothers, saying, "I am Joseph; is my father still alive?" At first, the brothers were speechless and were afraid of Joseph. But he reassured them that, notwithstanding their evil intent in selling him, God had sent him to Egypt to save their lives. (44:18 – 45:8)

Pharaoh's invitation. Joseph told his brothers to go home to Canaan and tell their father that Joseph asks his father to come to him in Egypt. When Pharaoh heard that Joseph's brothers had come, he immediately told Joseph to invite his entire family, and Pharaoh will give them the best land in Egypt. And, at Pharaoh's command, Joseph sent wagons to transport his brothers' wives and children to Egypt. When the brothers came home and delivered Joseph's message, Jacob at first didn't believe that Joseph was alive and was viceroy of Egypt; but when he realized the truth, his spirit revived, and he resolved to go to Egypt to see his son. (45:9–28)

The province of Goshen: Pharaoh's grant to the sons of Israel. Israel—the name by which the Torah now refers to Jacob—left his home with all his family and all his belongings. When he reached Beer-Sheba, God appeared to him in a dream and told him not to fear going to Egypt, because He will be with Jacob. Jacob and his family arrived in Egypt; and Pharaoh, true to his word, gave them prime land in the province of Goshen. (46:1 – 47:27)

Jacob's blessings. Jacob lived in Egypt for seventeen years. When Jacob was about to die, he blessed Joseph's two sons Manasseh and Ephraim. And Jacob said that both of them would henceforth be regarded as his own sons, equal to Reuben or Simeon in their inheritance; but any of Joseph's sons born after Jacob's arrival in Egypt would be regarded as Joseph's sons. Then Jacob called for all of his sons to be brought to him, and he blessed each of them before he died. Jacob died in Egypt at 147 years old. Joseph had Jacob's body mummified, and, in accordance with Jacob's wishes, Joseph brought the body to Canaan for burial in the Cave of Machpelah. (47:28 – 50:13)

Joseph's return to Egypt. When Joseph returned from burying his father, his brothers expected that Joseph would now exact revenge upon them for the evil they had done him. So they told him that Jacob, before he died, had commanded them to ask Joseph to forgive them. But Joseph reiterated his previous assertion, saying that although the brothers had had evil intentions, God's intentions were for good, to save many lives. (50:14–21)

Joseph's last days. Joseph lived in Egypt for many years, and he lived to see his grandsons. Before his death, Joseph had the sons of Israel swear to him that when God will eventually bring His people out of Egypt to the land of Canaan, they will take his body with them. Joseph died in Egypt at the age of 110 years. He was mummified and placed in a coffin. (50:22–26)

II. THE BOOK OF EXODUS (*Shemot*)

Enslavement of the Israelites. The clan of Israel that came to Egypt numbered seventy; but after the death of Joseph and his generation, their numbers increased greatly. A new king arose in Egypt, and, fearing the Israelites' growing numbers, he enslaved them. He oppressed the Hebrew slaves with hard work and with cruel decrees; and they built him two cities: Pithom and Ra'amses. But their numbers continued to increase. Pharaoh commanded the midwives that they must put to death every newborn male Hebrew. But two midwives, named Shifra and Puah, feared God, and they allowed the boys to live. Then, Pharaoh decreed that all male infants be drowned in the Nile. (Exodus, Chapter 1)

The birth of Moses. A certain Israelite couple had a newborn son. After hiding the baby for three months, the mother realized she couldn't hide him any longer. So she put her baby in a watertight basket and set him afloat on the Nile River; and the baby's sister watched from the distance, to see what would become of her little brother. (2:1–4)

Pharaoh's daughter. Pharaoh's daughter went with her slave-girls to bathe in the Nile, and she saw a basket among the reeds. Upon opening the basket, she saw a crying baby boy and immediately realized he was a Hebrew child. Then the baby's sister approached and offered to bring a wet-nurse; and she brought the baby's mother to nurse the baby for Pharaoh's daughter. In defiance of

Pharaoh's decree, Pharaoh's daughter adopted the baby as her own son and gave him the name Moses (*Moshe*). (2:5–10)

Escape to Midian. When Moses grew up, he went to see the suffering of his brothers; and he saw an Egyptian smiting a Hebrew man. Moses looked about, and, seeing nobody else around, he intervened. He killed the Egyptian, and he buried the body. On the following day, Moses realized that his act had been discovered, and Pharaoh was seeking to have him killed. So Moses fled Egypt and went to the land of Midian. There, at a well, he met the seven daughters of Re'uel the priest of Midian; and Moses rescued them from shepherds who had chased them away from the well. Re'uel—who was also known as Jethro (*Yitro*)—invited Moses to remain with him and gave him his eldest daughter Zipporah as his wife. She bore Moses a son named Gershom. (2:11–22)

The burning bush. Many years passed, and the king of Egypt died. Moses was tending his father-in-law Jethro's sheep when he came with his flock to Mount Horeb. There, an angel appeared to him in a burning bush, but the bush was not consumed. Moses approached, and God spoke to him, saying that He had heard the cries of the Israelites, and He commanded Moses to return to Egypt, to free the Israelites and bring them to the land of Canaan. Moses doubted his fitness for the job, but God assured Moses that He would be with him; and when Moses brings the people out of Egypt, they will worship God at that same mountain, Mount Horeb. (2:23 – 3:15)

Moses's mission. God told Moses to ask Pharaoh to allow the Israelites to go three days into the desert to worship the Lord; but, God said, Pharaoh will not let them go until God strikes Egypt with wondrous punishments. And, so that the Israelites would believe that the Lord had sent him, God gave Moses two signs. For the first sign, Moses put his hand into his bosom, and his hand turned leprous; he put his hand in again, and it was healed. For the second sign, God told Moses to throw his staff on the ground, and it changed into a snake; and when he seized the snake's tail, it changed back to a staff. Moses objected, saying that he had a speech impediment. God agreed to have Moses's brother Aaron speak for Moses. (3:16 – 4:17)

Moses's return to Egypt. Moses departed Midian. God sent Aaron to meet his brother Moses in the desert, and the two of them returned to Egypt together. They gathered the elders of Israel. Aaron told them that the Lord had heard their cries and would take them out of Egypt, and Moses showed the Israelites the two signs that God had given him. When Moses and Aaron came before Pharaoh and delivered God's command that he release the Israelites to worship the Lord in the desert, Pharaoh said, "Who is the Lord that I should listen to Him?" Not only did Pharaoh refuse to release the Israelites, but he increased their labor: no longer was straw given to them for making bricks, but they had to gather the straw themselves, while the daily quota of bricks that they had to make remained unchanged. Failure to meet the quota would result in beatings. Moses complained to God that sending him to Pharaoh had worsened the lot of the Hebrew slaves; but God answered Moses that he has yet to see what God will do to Pharaoh; and in the end, God said, Pharaoh will cast out the Israelites from his land with a strong hand. (4:18 – 6:1)

Moses and Aaron confront Pharaoh. God spoke to Moses and told him that He will fulfill the covenant He made with the Patriarchs. He will bring the Israelites out of Egypt and will give them the land that He promised to give them. God sent Moses and Aaron to speak to Pharaoh again, to tell him to release the Israelites from his land. Aaron threw down his staff before Pharaoh, and it turned into a serpent. Pharaoh called his sorcerers. They also threw down their staffs, and their staffs changed into serpents; but Aaron's staff swallowed all their staffs. Pharaoh's heart hardened, and he didn't listen to Moses and Aaron. (6:2 –7:13)

The first plague: Blood. At God's command, in the morning Moses and Aaron went to meet Pharaoh at the river bank. They told Pharaoh that the God of the Hebrews sent them to say that he must release the Hebrews. But Pharaoh continued to refuse. Aaron then took Moses's staff and, in front of Pharaoh, he struck the water of the Nile. The water changed to blood, in the Nile and in all the waterways, in the lakes and in the reservoirs. The Nile remained bloody for seven days, and all the fish in the river died. Pharaoh's sorcerers were also able to turn water to blood, and Pharaoh refused to release the Israelites. (7:14–25)

The second plague: Frogs. God again sent Moses and Aaron back to Pharaoh with God's command to release the Israelites; but again, Pharaoh refused. Therefore, as God commanded, Aaron raised his staff over the waters of Egypt, and frogs swarmed all over the land: in people's homes, in their beds, and even in their ovens. Pharaoh called for Moses and Aaron, and he agreed to release the Israelites to worship the Lord if Moses and Aaron will pray to God to remove the frogs from him and his people. Moses prayed to God; and on the following day, all the frogs died in the houses and in the fields. The stench of the dead frogs filled the land. And Pharaoh, seeing that the land was no longer filled with frogs, hardened his heart, and he again refused to release the Israelites. (7:26 – 8:11)

The third plague: Lice. At God's command, Aaron struck the ground with his staff, and lice afflicted all of Egypt. Pharaoh's sorcerers were unable to remove the lice, and they declared that this was a sign from God. But Pharaoh again refused to listen. (8:12–15)

The fourth plague: A horde of insects. Early in the morning, Moses met Pharaoh at the river and warned him that if he still refuses to release the Israelites, God will bring a horde of insects upon the land of Egypt, but not in the province of Goshen where the Israelites live. And so it was, and the country was ravaged. Pharaoh agreed to let the Israelites leave Egypt to worship the Lord in the desert, provided they do not go far. But when God removed the plague, Pharaoh again hardened his heart and refused to release the Israelites. (8:16–28)

The fifth plague: Pestilence. At God's command, Moses went to Pharaoh and told him that if he doesn't release the Israelites, God will bring a pestilence upon all the livestock of the Egyptians. And so, on the following morning, the Egyptian livestock died of a pestilence; but of the Israelites' animals, not a single one died. Still, Pharaoh refused to release the Israelites. (9:1–7)

The sixth and seventh plagues. God afflicted the Egyptians with boils that covered the bodies of the people and their remaining livestock. God strengthened Pharaoh's heart, and Pharaoh continued refusing to listen to God's command. God sent Moses back to Pharaoh to warn that on the following day there would be hail such as Egypt had never seen. Any animals or people left outside would die; and grass and trees would be destroyed. Moses raised his staff heavenwards, and a devastating hail struck the land of Egypt. Fire rained down from heaven, mixed with the hail. But in the province of Goshen, where the Israelites lived, there was no hail. Then Pharaoh agreed to let the Israelites leave; but when the hail stopped, he again strengthened his resolve and refused to let them go. (9:8–35)

The eighth and ninth plagues. For the eighth plague, God sent locusts to consume all the vegetation that had not been devastated by the hail. And for the ninth plague, there was profound darkness in Egypt for three days; but there was light where the Israelites dwelled. Pharaoh offered to allow the Israelites to go, on condition that they leave their sheep and their cattle behind. But Moses insisted that they must also take their livestock, and Pharaoh refused to let them go. (Chapter 10)

Preparation for the tenth plague. Moses warned that at midnight, God will strike every firstborn Egyptian dead, but no Israelite will die. Pharaoh, however, did not heed the warning and release the Israelites. On the Lord's instructions, Moses told the people of Israel that on the fourteenth day of that month they should slaughter a sheep or a goat and place its blood on the doorposts and lintel. They should roast the meat, and in the evening they should eat it along with *matzot*—unleavened bread—and with bitter herbs. All Israelites must stay within their homes until morning. And, Moses said, when God strikes Egypt at midnight, He will not allow death to strike at any home marked with blood on the doorposts. (11:1 – 12:28)

The tenth plague: Death of the Firstborn. Midnight arrived, and the Lord struck every Egyptian firstborn, both freeman and prisoner, both human and animal; and a great cry rose up in all of Egypt. Then Pharaoh called to Moses and Aaron. He ordered them to leave Egypt with all their people and their livestock. In accordance with Moses's instructions, the Israelites asked the Egyptians for gold and silver implements and for clothing. The Lord had caused the Egyptians to be well disposed to the Israelites, and the Egyptians gave them what they had requested. Thus, after a stay of 430 years, the Lord took the Israelites out of Egypt: 600,000 men, and their wives and children. All firstborn Israelites were to be dedicated to the Lord's service. And henceforth, the Lord decreed, Israelites must remember the redemption from Egypt. The day of the Exodus must be celebrated through all generations, as the day that God delivered His people from bondage in Egypt. For seven days, *matzot* should be eaten; and all Israelites must tell their children how the Lord killed all Egyptian firstborn, and how He brought the Israelites out of Egypt with a strong hand. (12:29 – 13:16)

The Israelites' departure, and Pharaoh's regret. When Pharaoh released the Israelites, God directed them through the desert, to the Sea of Reeds. Moses took the bones of Joseph with him, in fulfillment of the promise that the sons of Israel had made to Joseph. The Lord's presence went before the Israelites as a pillar of cloud by day and as a pillar of fire by night, to guide them on their way. And they camped opposite Baal-Zephon, by the sea. When Pharaoh was informed that the Israelites had departed, he had a change of heart and regretted that he had let them go. He harnessed his chariot and took with him all the chariots of Egypt, including six hundred elite chariots; and he caught up to the Israelites as they camped by the sea. When they saw the Egyptian cavalry approaching, the people feared greatly, and they demanded to return to Egypt. But Moses told them not to be afraid, because the Lord will fight for them against the Egyptians. (13:17 – 14:14)

The splitting of the sea. God's angel who was in front of the Israelite camp went behind them, and the pillar of cloud also went behind them, separating them from the Egyptians. At the Lord's command, Moses raised his staff over the sea, and the Lord sent a strong east wind over the water. The sea split, and the dry seabed was exposed. The Israelites crossed the sea on dry land through the night, and the water stood as a wall to their right and to their left. The entire Egyptian cavalry pursued the Israelites through the sea. Toward morning, the Lord told Moses to raise his hand over the sea, and the waters returned, drowning all the Egyptians who had entered the seabed. The people of Israel witnessed the Lord's mighty hand, and they put their trust in the Lord and in Moses. (14:15–31)

The Song of the Sea. When the people saw that they were saved, Moses led them in song, praising the Lord. And Miriam the prophetess, the sister of Moses, led the women singing the Lord's praises. (15:1–21)

Food and water in the desert. Leaving the Sea of Reeds, Moses led the people of Israel through the desert. Water was scarce, and the people longed for the plentiful meat and bread that they used to eat in Egypt. Moses assured his people that the Lord had heard their complaints, saying they will have meat in the evening and bread in the morning. So, that evening quail came, and the quail covered the camp. In the morning, when the dew fell, under the dew the people found a bread-like food. They didn't know what it was, and they said, *man hu*—what is it? Therefore they called it *man*—"Manna." From that day on, the Manna fell from heaven every morning except Saturday; and on Fridays there was a double amount. The Israelites continued to eat the Manna for forty years, until they arrived at the border of Canaan. (15:22 – 16:36)

Moses and the rock. The Israelites traveled onward through the desert, and they camped at a place called Rephidim. There, they were short of water, and they began to complain and argue with Moses, demanding water and saying, "Why did you take us out of Egypt to die in the desert?" At the Lord's direction, Moses struck a rock with his staff. Water came out of the rock, and there was enough for the people and their livestock to drink. Moses re-named the place *Massa Um'riva*—Testing and Disputation. (17:1–7)

Amalek. While still camped at Rephidim, the Amalekites came and attacked the people of Israel; and the Israelite army, with Joshua in command, defeated Amalek. (17:8–16)

Jethro. Jethro, Priest of Midian, the father-in-law of Moses, heard of all the miracles that God had performed for Israel. Jethro took Moses's wife and two sons—Gershom and Eliezer—and brought them to Moses, to where the Israelites were camped near Mount Horeb. Jethro saw that Moses was sitting in judgement from early morning until the evening. He advised Moses to appoint judges to decide routine matters, and only the difficult cases should be referred to Moses. Moses followed Jethro's advice; and Jethro returned to his home. (Chapter 18)

The Ten Commandments—The Decalogue. In the third month after the Israelites left Egypt, they arrived at Mount Horeb, also known as Mount Sinai. God told Moses to assemble the nation at the foot of the mountain; and—amidst thunder and lightning and the sound of a *shofar*—God spoke the Decalogue to all the people: 1) I am the Lord your God, who took you out of the land of Egypt, out of the house of slavery. 2) Do not have another god beside me, and do not bow down to or worship another god. 3) Do not take the name of the Lord in vain. 4) Remember the Sabbath day—the seventh day, Saturday—and make it holy. 5) Honor your father and your mother. 6) Do not murder. 7) Do not commit adultery. 8) Do not steal. 9) Do not testify falsely against your fellow man. 10) Do not covet another person's house, or his wife, or his slaves, his animals, or any of his possessions. (Chapters 19 & 20)

Civil and criminal laws. God presented Moses with a set of laws, comprising laws in the following categories:

> Laws pertaining to the Hebrew bondman, who is released from servitude after six years. The Hebrew bondman's rights and his master's obligations are specified.
>
> Murder and accidental homicide.
>
> Crimes against parents.
>
> Kidnapping, which, like murder, is a capital crime.
>
> Laws pertaining to personal injury, including that the penalty for causing an injury must be commensurate with the nature of the injury.
>
> Injuries caused by a person's animal.
>
> Property damage caused by a person's animal or due to negligence.
>
> Laws pertaining to penalty and restitution for theft.
>
> Laws pertaining to safekeeping, including accidental loss or embezzlement of a deposit.
>
> Laws pertaining to seduction, witchcraft, and sodomy.
>
> Loans, and pledges taken as security.
>
> Laws pertaining to the administration of justice, including impartiality of judges, the prohibition of taking bribes, and

the requirement to distance oneself from falsehood.

The prohibition against oppressing a stranger, because you were strangers in Egypt and you understand the soul of the stranger.

And following this set of civil and criminal laws, the Torah lists the three pilgrimage festivals that all Israelites are to celebrate: the festival of *matzot* that commemorates the Exodus from Egypt; the grain harvest festival; and the harvest festival at the end of the agricultural year. (21:1 – 23:19)

The Promised Land. God reiterated His promise that He will bring the Israelites to the land of Canaan. He delineated the borders of the Promised Land. And He warned the Israelites not to worship any of the Canaanite deities. (23:20–33)

The tablets of the Decalogue. (Chapter 24: see below, following Chapter 31.)

Instructions for building the Tabernacle. At the Lord's direction, Moses collected donations from the people for building the Tabernacle (the *Mishkan*)—a tent in which the Lord's Presence will be manifest. God gave Moses detailed instructions regarding the construction of the Tabernacle that Moses would soon supervise, and the implements that were to be within the Tabernacle. These included the Ark into which will be placed the tablets of the Decalogue that God will give Moses; the curtains, the altar, and the Menorah—a solid gold seven-branched candelabra, which Aaron and his sons will light daily using the purest olive oil. (25:1 – 27:21)

The priestly garments. God commanded Moses to fashion priestly garments for Aaron and his sons. Aaron's garments included a headdress, a robe, a breastplate, and a sash, and two chains of pure gold. The garments were to be decorated with gold, and with blue, purple, and crimson threads. The breastplate was to be made of gold, of blue, purple, and crimson threads, and twisted linen; and in the breastplate were to be set twelve gemstones arranged in four rows, corresponding to the twelve tribes of Israel. Aaron, the High Priest, would use the breastplate when he consulted the Lord for judgement regarding the people of Israel. (Chapter 28)

Consecration of Aaron and his sons. God commanded Moses that when the Tabernacle is built and the priestly garments are completed, Moses is to bring Aaron and his sons to the entrance of the Tent of Meeting—the Tabernacle—and wash them with water. Moses will dress Aaron in his priestly garments and anoint him as High Priest. Moses will dress Aaron's sons in their priestly garments, and the priesthood will be theirs for all time. And, the Lord told Moses, Aaron's sacred garments will be passed on to his son who will succeed him as High Priest. Finally, the Lord told Moses to offer a sacrifice to inaugurate the Tabernacle. (29:1–37)

The Tabernacle ritual. The Lord told Moses that when the Tabernacle is completed, a burnt offering will be brought twice daily near the entrance of the Tent of Meeting, in the morning and at twilight; and the Lord will speak to Moses there. In the sanctuary, in front of the curtain that is near the Ark of the Covenant, there will be a small incense-altar, on which Aaron will burn a fragrant incense every morning and every evening. (29:38 – 30:10)

The census, and the Tabernacle service. The Lord commanded Moses to take a census by having every man of age at least twenty years contribute a half shekel toward the construction and maintenance of the Tabernacle. Then the Lord commanded

Moses to make a wash-basin for Aaron and his sons to wash their hands and feet on entering the Tent of Meeting. And the Lord instructed Moses regarding the anointing oil that will be used to anoint the Tabernacle and the Ark of the Covenant. (30:11–38)

Bezalel. God told Moses to appoint Bezalel of the tribe of Judah to be the artisan in charge of making the gold and silver, copper, stone, and wooden implements for the Tabernacle; and God will imbue Bezalel with wisdom and with skill to perform that task. And Oholiav of the tribe of Dan will be Bezalel's assistant in constructing the Tabernacle. (31:1–11)

Sabbath observance. All of Israel must keep the Sabbath, as a sign of the covenant between the Lord and Israel throughout the generations. For six days they may work, but the seventh day of the week is holy, and no work may be done. (31:12–17)

The tablets of the Decalogue. Moses, along with Aaron and his sons Nadab (*Nadav*) and Abihu (*Avihu*), and seventy elders, went up the mountain, and there they had a vision of God. Then, when God called him, Moses alone ascended further and entered the cloud that covered the mountain, in order to receive the two tablets of the Decalogue. Moses remained on the mountain for forty days and forty nights. (Chapter 24)

The Golden Calf. When God finished speaking to Moses on Mount Sinai, He gave Moses the two stone tablets of the covenant. But meanwhile, when Moses had been on the mountain for a long time, the Israelites doubted that he would return. They demanded that Aaron make a golden calf, and they contributed their gold jewelry for making the idol. When the idol was completed, the people worshipped the Golden Calf, saying, "This is the god that brought you out of the land of Egypt." And they ate and drank and reveled before the idol. (32:1–6)

Breaking the tablets. God told Moses that his people had made and worshipped an idol. God threatened to annihilate them and make a new nation from Moses. But Moses prayed to God and asked Him to forgive His nation, and not to break the covenant that He had made with the Patriarchs. God accepted Moses's prayer, and Moses descended the mountain carrying the two tablets. When Moses saw the calf and the people dancing, he became enraged, and he hurled the tablets, smashing them at the foot of the mountain. Moses destroyed the calf and decreed the death penalty for the 3,000 men who had worshipped the idol. And Moses again asked the Lord to forgive the grievous sin that the nation had committed. (32:7–35)

Moses's tent outside the camp. Because of their recent infraction, God declared the people unworthy to have the Lord's presence among them. Therefore, Moses pitched a tent outside the camp, where people could go to seek the Lord. When Moses went there, the pillar of cloud would descend at the tent's entrance; and the Lord would speak to Moses. (33:1–11)

Moses's vision of God. Moses asked God to allow him to see God's glory. God answered that no person can see God's face and live; but He will put Moses in the cleft of a rock and shield his vision; and Moses will only see the Lord from behind. (33:12–23)

The second set of tablets. At the Lord's direction, Moses carved two new stone tablets and ascended the mountain. There, God inscribed the new tablets with the Decalogue, reaffirming His covenant with the nation of Israel. Moses now appealed to the Lord's attributes of mercy and compassion, and again asked the

Lord to forgive His people for their sin. And again he requested that the Lord continue to have His presence in the midst of the people. The Lord reiterated His promise to bring the Israelites to the land of Canaan, but He warned them not to worship another god, and not to make treaties with or intermarry with the Canaanites. The people of Israel must not adopt Canaanite worship but must celebrate the three pilgrimage festivals that God has commanded, and they must not cook a young goat in its mother's milk. Moses again remained on Mount Sinai for forty days and forty nights. When he descended the mountain, the skin of his face glowed, and the people were afraid to approach him. Therefore, Moses put a veil over his face; and he removed the veil when he went to speak with God. (Chapter 34)

Construction of the Tabernacle. Moses assembled the people and told them to build the Tabernacle according to the instructions that God previously had given him. He appointed Bezalel and Oholiav to supervise the project. And the Israelites made the Tabernacle and all its implements and vessels, and all the priestly garments for Aaron and his sons, in accordance with the Lord's instructions to Moses. (35:1 – 39:32)

Completion and dedication of the Tabernacle. When the Tabernacle was completed, Moses blessed the people. As the Lord commanded, Moses dressed Aaron in his priestly garments and anointed him High Priest. Then he dressed Aaron's sons in their tunics and anointed them for everlasting priesthood. On the first day of the first month of the second year, the completed Tabernacle was erected. The cloud covered it, and the Lord's glory filled the Tabernacle. Whenever the cloud lifted from above the Tabernacle, the people of Israel would resume their journey, and when the cloud remained upon the Tabernacle, they would remain encamped. The Lord's cloud was over the Tabernacle by day, and a fire by night, throughout their travels. (39:33 – 40:38)

III. THE BOOK OF LEVITICUS (*Vayikra*)

The sacrificial laws. God called to Moses from within the Tent of Meeting and told him the laws pertaining to the sacrificial offerings that would be brought in the Tabernacle. There were burnt offerings of cattle, sheep, goats, doves, or pigeons. There were offerings of flour mixed with oil and incense, as well as personal sin-offerings, communal sin-offerings, and sin-offerings for a tribal chieftain who had sinned. The good-will offerings and gratitude offerings were in part burnt on the altar, in part given to the *kohen*—the priest—to eat, and in part eaten by the person offering the sacrifice. But a person could not partake of the sacrifice if he was ritually impure, for example if he had contacted a human corpse and had not yet been purified. God commanded that the people of Israel may not eat the meat of an animal that died a natural death or was killed by predators; and God forbade the Israelites to eat blood. (Leviticus, Chapters 1–7)

Moses consecrates Aaron and his sons. Moses dressed Aaron and his sons in their priestly garments and consecrated them as the Lord had instructed him (see Exodus, Chapter 29). Moses anointed the Tabernacle, its altar, and its implements, and he brought sacrificial offerings to inaugurate and consecrate the Tabernacle. He brought another sacrifice to consecrate Aaron and his sons, and he gave them their portion of the sacrifice to eat. (Chapter 8)

The eighth day. On the eighth day of the consecration period, Moses called to Aaron and his sons. He told Aaron to bring a sin-offering of a bull calf for himself, and additional burnt offerings for himself and on behalf of the people. Aaron raised his hands and blessed the nation; and a short while later, Moses and Aaron together blessed the people. The glory of the Lord appeared to the entire nation, and a fire descended from heaven, consuming the offering that was on the altar. The people saw, and they fell on their faces. (Chapter 9)

An alien fire. Nadab and Abihu, Aaron's two oldest sons, each took his fire-pan and placed fire and incense upon it. They brought into the Tabernacle an alien fire that the Lord had not commanded, and they offered the alien fire to the Lord. Thereupon, a fire descended from heaven and consumed them, and they died. (10:1–7)

Prohibition of intoxication on entering the Tabernacle. The Lord spoke to Aaron and warned him that he and his sons must not drink wine or beer before they enter the Tent of Meeting, lest they die. (10:8–11)

The dietary laws. The Lord spoke to Moses and Aaron and told them to tell the people of Israel which animals they may eat. Domestic animals that have split hooves and chew their cud, water-life having both fins and scales, and certain foul may be eaten. Certain grasshoppers and crickets may also be eaten, but all reptiles and other creeping animals are unclean and must not be eaten. (Chapter 11)

Laws pertaining to pregnancy. The Lord gave Moses laws regarding ritual impurity related to the period after delivering a baby. Also, a woman was to bring a sacrifice after delivering a baby. (Chapter 12)

Leprosy. The Lord gave Moses and Aaron laws pertaining to ritual impurity due to certain afflictions of the skin including *tzaraat*—leprosy. (Chapters 13–15)

***Yom Kippur*—the Day of Atonement.** After the death of Aaron's two sons, the Lord said that Aaron may not enter the holiest part of the Tabernacle—the Holy of Holies—at any time of Aaron's choosing. The Lord specified the details of the service of *Yom Kippur*. Aaron was to bring sacrifices to atone first for his own sins and those of his family, and then for the entire nation. Aaron was to take two goats and draw lots to determine which goat would be sacrificed to the Lord as a sin-offering. He was to place his hands on the other goat's head and symbolically put the sins of the people of Israel on its head. That goat was led into the desert, carrying the nation's sins with it. And it shall be an eternal law that on that day, the tenth day of the seventh month, all Israelites will fast, and no work must be done on that day; because on that day they will be purified of sins they committed against the Lord. (Chapter 16)

Prohibition of sacrifices outside the Tabernacle. God told Moses to tell Aaron and all the people of Israel that they may not slaughter any animals outside the Tabernacle. After slaughtering the animal in the Tabernacle, a portion was to be brought to the *kohen* as an offering on the altar, and only then would the person be allowed to eat the animal's meat. But the blood must not be eaten. (Chapter 17)

Forbidden relationships. The Lord told Moses that the people of Israel must not follow the abhorrent practices of Egypt or of the Canaanites whose land they will enter; but they are to live by the laws that the Lord commands. Various sexual relationships are forbidden, and child sacrifice is forbidden. (Chapter 18)

Be holy. The Lord told Moses to speak to the Israelites and tell them to be holy. Every person is to revere his mother and father, and keep the Sabbath. The people of Israel must be honest in business, have respect for and love of other people, uphold equal justice for all, treat the stranger as they would treat their own, refrain from gossip, pay employees on time, worship God, and they must not worship other deities. It is forbidden to mutilate or tattoo one's body, to employ a medium or necromancer, or to offer up one's child to the idol Molekh. And adultery and incest are forbidden. The people of Israel must not follow the Canaanite practices that were loathsome to the Lord, lest Israel be expelled from the land. Israel must be different from the other nations of the world. They must be holy, because God is holy and has declared Israel to be His. (Chapters 19 & 20)

Laws pertaining to the priests. A *kohen* must not become defiled by contact with a dead body, and he must not marry a divorced woman. A *kohen* who is ritually impure because of leprosy, certain discharges, or contact with a reptile may not eat of the sacrificial offerings until he is purified. Only a *kohen* and his family may eat the portion of a sacrificial offering that is given to the priest. The daughter of a *kohen* who marries a non-*kohen* may not eat the priestly portion; but if she is divorced or widowed and has no children, and she returns to live with her father, she may again eat the priestly portion of the sacrifices. (Chapters 21 & 22)

The holy days. The Lord spoke to Moses and told him to tell the people of Israel the particulars of the holy days; and foremost among them is the Sabbath. Work may be done for six days, but the seventh day of the week—the Sabbath—is holy to the Lord, and no work may be done. The Passover festival begins at twilight on the fourteenth day of the first month—the month that is now called *Nissan*. *Matzot* are eaten for seven days, and no work may be done on the first day and the seventh day. Once the Israelites have entered the land that the Lord will give them, seven weeks should be counted from the second day of the Passover festival. Then, on the fiftieth day, no work may be done. It will be a holy day, on which an offering of flour from the grain harvest will be brought. When a field is harvested, a corner of the field must not be reaped; but it should be left for the poor to gather the grain. The first day of the seventh month—the month that is now called *Tishrei*—will be a day of remembrance, a holy day on which a horn—the *shofar*—will be sounded. And the tenth day of that month will be a Day of Atonement—*Yom Kippur*—a day on which atonement is made before the Lord. It is a Sabbath of Sabbaths, a fast day on which no work may be done. The fifteenth day of the seventh month—*Tishrei*—starts the festival of *Sukkot*, at the time of harvesting the produce of the land. The first day of the festival and the eighth day are holy days, on which no work may be done. For seven days the people must dwell in huts—*sukkot*—to commemorate the huts in which the Israelites dwelled when the Lord brought them out of Egypt. These are all the festivals of the Lord, which Moses conveyed to the people of Israel. (Chapter 23)

The man who cursed the Lord. A man of mixed lineage, the son of an Egyptian father and an Israelite mother, fought with an Israelite man and publicly cursed God by name. Witnesses to the half-Egyptian man's blasphemy brought him before Moses, and Moses asked God to decide the punishment. God answered that anybody who curses God by name, whether an Israelite or an alien, shall be put to death. Also, God said, a murderer is to be put to death, but one who kills an animal shall pay, in proportion to the value of the animal's life. Whoever injures another person, a proportionate penalty shall be imposed upon him—an eye for an eye, a tooth for a tooth. And there must be one law for all: the same for an alien as for a citizen. (Chapter 24)

The sabbatical year and the jubilee. When still at Mount Sinai, the Lord told Moses that when the Israelites enter the Promised Land, every seventh year will be a sabbath for the land. On that year, fields must not be worked, and the harvest must not be reaped. And after every seven cycles of sabbatical years, the fiftieth year will be a jubilee (*Yovel*). The jubilee year will be ushered in by blowing a *shofar*—a ram's horn—on the Day of Atonement, proclaiming liberty throughout the land. All Hebrew bondmen will be liberated, ancestral land will revert to its original owners, and fields will not be worked during the jubilee year. (25:1–34)

Poverty, loans, and the Hebrew bondman. If a fellow Israelite is in financial difficulty and you give him a loan, you may not charge him interest. If a fellow Israelite is impoverished and sells himself as a bondman, it is forbidden to work him as a slave. He must be treated as a resident employee; and he must go free in the jubilee year. But non-Israelites may be bought as slaves. If an Israelite is impoverished and is sold as a slave to a non-Israelite residing in the land, it is incumbent upon the Israelite slave's relatives to redeem him from slavery, but they must pay the non-Israelite owner fair compensation. (25:35 – 26:2)

Reward and punishment. God promised that if the people of Israel follow His laws and observe His commandments, the land will be fertile, and there will be peace in the land. God's presence will be in the midst of the people of Israel, and He will not expel His nation; for He is the Lord God of Israel, Who brought them out of slavery and established them as a nation. Conversely, if the people of Israel reject God's laws and have contempt for His precepts, He will afflict them with diseases, and they will flee before their enemies. If the people do not heed those initial warnings, God will inflict upon them more severe punishments; and if they continue in their wicked actions, there will be still more severe penalties. If the nation still persists in its rebellious ways, the cities will be devastated, and Israel will be exiled among the nations. But even then, the Lord will not reject them, and He will not dissolve His covenant with them. When they are in the lands of their enemies, they will realize their sin and will expiate their guilt. And the Lord will keep to His covenant that He made with Israel when He took them out of Egypt. This concludes the conditions of the covenant that the Lord made with the people of Israel at Mount Sinai. (26:3–46)

Voluntary contributions. The book of Leviticus ends with laws pertaining to voluntary contributions that people will make to the Sanctuary, and laws pertaining to tithes, which are one tenth of a farmer's produce or of animals that are born in the farmer's herd. (Chapter 27)

IV. THE BOOK OF NUMBERS (*Bamidbar*)

The census. On the first day of the second month of the second year after the Exodus of the people of Israel from Egypt, the Lord commanded Moses to take a census of all males of military age, grouped by their tribes and by their clans. The total, excluding the Levites, was 603,550. The Levites—who were not counted among the tribes—did not serve in the army, but they guarded the Tabernacle and maintained it, and they camped around the Tabernacle. Each of the twelve tribes camped by its banner, three tribes on each side of the Levite camp. The tribe of Judah camped to the east; and when the Israelites traveled through the desert, they would lead. When the Tabernacle traveled through the desert, the Levites dismantled it, and when the Israelites encamped, the Levites erected it again. (Numbers, Chapters 1 & 2)

The Levites. Of the Levites, the priestly class consisted of Aaron and his descendants. Aaron's two oldest sons, Nadab and Abihu, died when they brought an alien fire into the Tabernacle; and Aaron's two remaining sons, Eleazar and Ithamar, served in their stead during their father's lifetime. God ordained that the Levites would substitute for the firstborn Israelites in the Lord's service, and He ordered Moses to take a census of the Levites from the age of one month and older. The Levites numbered 22,000. Levites from age thirty to fifty were assigned duties in the Tent of Meeting, and the three clans of Levites were assigned different duties. (Chapters 3 & 4)

Maintenance of purity. The Lord told Moses to maintain the purity of the Israelites' camp by having all people afflicted with leprosy or with other types of ritual impurity sent to a place outside the camp. And so it was done. (Chapter 5)

The nazirite. A man or a woman may voluntarily take an oath to become a "nazirite" for a specified period of time. The nazirite may not drink wine or beer, nor have any form of grapes. And the nazirite may not cut his hair or become ritually impure even for the death of a parent. At the conclusion of the specified time, the nazirite brings a sin-offering and other sacrifices; he shaves his head, and he drinks wine. (6:1–21)

The priestly blessing. The Lord told Moses the words that Aaron and his sons were to use to transmit the Lord's blessing to the people of Israel. (6:22–27)

Completion of the Tabernacle. When the Tabernacle was completed, Moses anointed it, and all its implements, and its altar. Then each of the twelve tribal chieftains brought burnt offerings to the Tabernacle, one chieftain on each day. At the conclusion of their offerings, when Moses entered the Tent of Meeting, he heard the voice of God speaking with him from above the curtain that covered the Ark. (Chapter 7)

The Menorah and the Levites. Moses made the Menorah, the solid gold seven-branched candelabra, in accordance with the vision that the Lord had shown him; and he told Aaron how to light the candles. God instructed Moses how to purify the Levites to serve in the Tabernacle. From the day that God smote the firstborn of Egypt, the firstborn of Israel were consecrated to the service of the Lord, but the Lord chose the Levites to replace the firstborn;

and of the Levites, Aaron and his descendants were chosen to be the priests and to atone for the sins of the people. (Chapter 8)

The second Passover festival. In the second year after leaving Egypt, when it came time to celebrate the Passover festival, there were some who were ritually impure and therefore couldn't bring the Passover offering. In order not to deprive them of celebrating the holiday, God told Moses that henceforth anybody who, because of ritual impurity or because he is far away, is unable to celebrate Passover at its proper time, that person may bring the Passover offering and celebrate the festival one month later. (9:1–14)

The cloud and the fire. From the day the Tabernacle was completed, a cloud covered the Tabernacle by day, and the appearance of fire was on it by night, until morning. Whenever the cloud lifted off the Tabernacle, the people of Israel would travel through the desert; and wherever the cloud came to rest, there they would make camp. Thus, whether the cloud lingered for only one day or for many months, it was only by God's will that the nation would travel onwards. (9:15–23)

The silver trumpets. The Lord commanded Moses to make two silver trumpets, which would be used to summon the people to assembly, and to announce the resumption of travel through the desert. When the people are settled in their land, the trumpets will also be used to summon the nation to battle against an attacker. And the trumpets will be sounded on festivals. (10:1–10)

The nation journeys onward. On the twentieth day of the second month—the month that is now called *Iyyar*—in the second year from the Exodus, the cloud lifted off the Tabernacle, and the nation left Mount Sinai to travel through the desert. Moses asked his father-in-law to accompany the Israelites to the land that the

Lord promised them, but his father-in-law said he would go home to Midian. Moses again entreated him to remain with Israel, saying that he would be their eyes in the desert, and he would be treated well in the new land. But the Torah is silent about whether he remained with Israel or returned to Midian. (10:11–36)

A craving for meat. After a three-day journey through the desert, the nation made camp; and shortly thereafter, the people began to complain. The rabble-rousers—these were Egyptians who had voluntarily gone with the Israelites when they left Egypt—remembered all the good foods they had in Egypt, and they demanded that Moses give them meat to eat. The Israelites then took up the complaint and said they were tired of the Manna. Moses cried out to the Lord about the burden that God had placed on him to lead the nation, and he asked God where he would get meat to feed the entire nation. (11:1–15)

The seventy elders. The Lord told Moses to select seventy of the elders of Israel, and bring them to the Tent of Meeting. There, God said, He will distribute some of Moses's spirit among them, so that they will share the burden of leadership with Moses. (11:16–17)

The people get their meat. At the Lord's command, Moses told the people that because they complained, the Lord will provide them with meat; but they will have the meat for thirty days, until it is coming out of their noses. The Lord sent a wind from the sea, and it carried a large flock of quail. The quail landed in and around the camp, and the people gathered up the quail in large numbers. (11:18–35)

Moses's Nubian wife. Moses's sister Miriam gossiped with Aaron about Moses regarding a Nubian woman whom Moses had married; and they said that God speaks not only to Moses but to them as well. The Lord suddenly summoned Moses, Aaron, and Miriam to the Tent of Meeting. There He reprimanded Miriam and Aaron for speaking badly of Moses, and God declared that Moses is unique among prophets. To other prophets, God speaks in dreams and in riddles; but to Moses, He speaks clearly. When God's presence departed, Aaron saw that Miriam was afflicted with leprosy. Moses cried out to the Lord and prayed for Him to heal Miriam. The Lord told Moses that Miriam should be isolated outside the camp for seven days, and then she will be healed. And when the seven days were completed, the nation resumed its journey. (Chapter 12)

Spies. The Lord told Moses to select one person from each tribe and send them to Canaan to scout out the land that God is giving to the people of Israel; and Moses selected the chieftain of each tribe. He told them to assess the land and its people, and he asked them to report whether the people of Canaan are strong or weak, whether they are few or numerous, whether they live in the open or in fortifications; and whether the land is fertile or lean, good or bad. When the men returned after forty days, ten of the twelve reported that the land was too well fortified and the people too strong to conquer; and, moreover, they had seen giants there. That night, the people wept, and many wanted to return to Egypt. But two of the spies, Joshua and Caleb, disagreed. They declared that, with the Lord's help, the Israelites will indeed conquer, and that the land is very, very good. The people were about to stone Joshua and Caleb, and they were only prevented when the presence of the Lord became manifest. (13:1 – 14:10)

The aftermath of the spies' report. The Lord asked Moses how long the people will reject Him and will not have faith in Him, despite all He has done for them; and He proposed to wipe them out with a plague and to make a new, even greater nation from Moses. Moses replied that if God were to do so, the Egyptians and other nations would say that God did not have the power to bring the Israelites to the land that He had promised them. Moses prayed to the Lord, whose foremost attributes are mercy and compassion, to forgive His nation and not to wipe them out; and the Lord consented. But, God said, this was now the tenth time that the people had tested Him. The Israelites will be condemned to remain in the desert for forty years—one year for each of the forty days that the spies scouted the land. All the people who had seen God's wonders but nevertheless rebelled against Him will die in the desert, and only their children will see the Promised Land. And the ten spies who had reported unfavorably about the land—all the spies except for Joshua and Caleb—died in a pestilence. (14:11–45)

Tzitzit. The Lord spoke to Moses and told him to tell the people of Israel that henceforth throughout the generations they shall put *tzitzit*—tassels—on the corners of their garments, including one blue thread, to remind them of the Lord's commandments, to prevent them from following the dictates of their hearts and of their eyes, and so that they shall be holy to the Lord their God. (Chapter 15)

Korah's rebellion. Korah, a cousin of Moses and Aaron, gathered 250 clan leaders and other prominent people. They challenged the leadership of Moses and Aaron and the selection of Aaron to be High Priest, a position that Korah wanted for himself. Moses replied that God will determine who should be High Priest, and Moses challenged Korah to a test. Moses told Korah and all his followers to put fire and incense in their pans and offer it to the Lord; and the one whom the Lord will choose will be High Priest. Korah agreed to the test, but the result came out in Aaron's favor. Moses told the people to separate themselves from the rebels. The earth opened up and swallowed Korah and his household; and a fire descended from heaven and consumed Korah's 250 followers. (Chapter 16)

Accusations, and a pestilence. On the following day, the people railed against Moses and Aaron, holding them responsible for the deaths of Korah's followers; and God unleashed a plague upon the rebellious people. But as soon as the plague began, Moses told Aaron to take fire from the altar and put it on his fire-pan, along with incense, and go out among the people to atone for them. Aaron did so. He ran into the midst of the people, standing between the dead and the living, and the plague ceased. (17:1–15)

Reaffirmation of Aaron's priestly leadership, and the Levites' status. In order to silence the people's murmurings, the Lord told Moses to take the staff of each tribal chieftain and write the tribe's name on it, and to take Aaron's staff to represent the Levites. Moses was to place all the staffs in the Tent of Meeting, and whichever person the Lord would choose, his staff would blossom. Moses did so; and the next morning, Aaron's staff had blossomed and borne fruit. The Lord then spoke to Moses and reaffirmed the privileges and duties of the *kohanim*—the priests, Aaron's descendants— and of the other Levites in the Tabernacle. And the Lord told Aaron that when the Promised Land is apportioned among the tribes, the Levites will not be assigned territory. But the people of Israel will be required to give the firstborn of their livestock and other gifts to the *kohanim*, and they will give one-tenth of their produce to the Levites. (17:16 – 18:32)

The red cow. The Lord told Moses and Aaron to have the people bring them a red cow without blemish. The cow was slaughtered, and burned together with cedarwood, hyssop, and crimson material; and the ashes were put away for safekeeping, for use in purifying people who become ritually impure. Any Israelite who came in contact with a human corpse had to immerse himself in water on the third day but would remain ritually unclean for seven days, after which he would be purified by being sprinkled with water containing some of the red cow's ashes. An unclean person was not to enter the Tabernacle until he was purified. (Chapter 19)

The death of Miriam, and Moses's sin. Many years passed, and the nation arrived at Kadesh. Miriam died there, and she was buried in the desert. There was no water for the people to drink, and they argued with Moses, saying, "Why did you take us out of Egypt to bring us to this evil place," to die in the desert? The Lord told Moses to take his staff and assemble the nation. Moses and Aaron were to speak to a rock and bring forth water from the rock. So Moses and Aaron assembled the nation; and Moses, calling the people rebels, struck the rock twice with his staff, although God had not told him to strike the rock. A lot of water streamed out: enough water for the people and their livestock. But God spoke to Moses and Aaron, saying that because they had failed to sanctify Him before the eyes of the people, they would not live to bring the nation to the land that God had promised them. (20:1–13)

Edom. Moses sent emissaries to the king of Edom, requesting permission for the Israelites to pass through his territory. Moses promised that his people would stay on the King's Road—which was an international highway for caravans—and that the Israelites would pay for any water that they or their livestock would drink. But the king refused to let them pass, and he mobilized his army. So the Israelites turned away from Edom. (20:14–21)

The death of Aaron. The Israelites left Kadesh and came to Mount Hor, near the border of Edom. There, Aaron died, and his son Eleazar became High Priest in his stead. The nation mourned Aaron for thirty days. (20:22–29)

The king of Arad. The Canaanite king of Arad, which was in the Negev, received reports of Israel's movement. He attacked the Israelites and took captives. Israel counterattacked and laid waste to his territory, taking no booty. (21:1–3)

Snakes. From Mount Hor, the nation went around Edom, and the people grew impatient. They complained that there was no food or water, and they loathed "the wretched bread"—the Manna. They were then attacked by poisonous snakes, and many died. The people begged forgiveness, and the Lord told Moses to make a copper serpent and put it up on a standard as a symbol. Whoever was bitten and looked up at the copper serpent would survive. (21:4–10)

Sihon and Og. The Israelites journeyed onwards and camped across from Arnon, which was in the desert between Moab and the Amorites. Israel sent emissaries to the Amorite king Sihon, requesting permission to pass through his territory. They promised to keep to the King's Road and not to drink any of the Amorites' water. But Sihon refused, and he attacked the Israelites. Israel defeated him in battle and seized his territory, including the Amorite capital Heshbon and all its suburbs. And Israelites settled in the Amorite land. Then Og, king of Bashan, came out to do battle with Israel. But Israel defeated him and seized his territory. The people of Israel journeyed onward and camped in the plains of Moab, on the banks of the Jordan, across from Jericho. (21:11 – 22:1)

Balak. Balak, king of Moab, heard what Israel had done to the Amorites, and he was very much afraid, because of the Israelites' great numbers. So, after conferring with the Midianites, Balak sent Moabite and Midianite elders to the prophet Balaam (*Bil'am*), who lived in Aram by the Euphrates River, asking Balaam to curse the Israelites. When God refused to allow Balaam to go, Balak sent still more distinguished officials and promised Balaam great honor. In a dream, God told Balaam that He will allow Balaam to go, but Balaam will speak only the words that God puts into his mouth. (22:2–20)

Balaam and the donkey. Balaam saddled his donkey, a she-ass, and he set out on his journey to Moab. On the way, in a narrow mountain pass, an angel stood in his way, blocking the path. The donkey saw the angel standing with drawn sword, and the donkey stopped. Balaam, however, didn't see the angel, and he struck the donkey three times. God opened the donkey's mouth, and she asked Balaam why he had hit her three times. Balaam finally saw the angel, and the angel warned him again that he will do only what God tells him to do. (22:21–38)

Balaam and Balak. Balaam arrived in Moab. He told Balak to set up seven altars and offer sacrifices. God appeared to Balaam and put words into his mouth; but it was a blessing and not the curse that Balak had expected. And, Balaam declared, Israel is unique, dwells alone, and is separate from all other nations. Balak was annoyed, but Balaam said he could only speak the words that God puts in his mouth. So Balak took Balaam to another location, hoping that God would let him curse from there; but again, Balaam blessed Israel. Balak took Balaam to a third location, but Balaam declared that whoever blesses Israel will be blessed, and whoever curses them will be cursed; and Balaam uttered yet another blessing. Balak got angry and expelled Balaam from his land. But before leaving, Balaam prophesied to Balak what will befall his nation in the latter days. Then Balaam went home to Aram. (22:39 – 24:25)

Debauchery with Moabite and Midianite women. Many people of Israel succumbed to Moabite harlots, who enticed them to participate in the rituals of their gods. Israelites feasted and worshipped the idol Baal-Peor, and God unleashed a plague against the people of Israel. Moses commanded that all those who participated in the rites of Baal-Peor be put to death. Just then, an Israelite clan chief came forward and flaunted his Midianite woman—the daughter of a Midianite chieftain—before Moses and all the people. While the elders stood dumbfounded and stunned into inaction, Phineas (*Pinchas*), the son of Eleazar the High Priest, rose from among the people, grabbed a spear, and ran them through—both the Israelite man and his Midianite woman. And the plague immediately stopped. The number of people who died in the plague totaled 24,000. (25:1–9 & 14–15)

God praises Phineas. The Lord spoke to Moses and praised Phineas for his quick and decisive action in an emergency, when the authorities had failed to act. And the Lord declared that He will grant Phineas and his descendants the priesthood in perpetuity. (25:10–13)

The Midianites. God told Moses to regard the Midianites as enemies and punish them, because they had instigated the plot to entice the Israelites to worship Baal-Peor, and because of the incident involving the Midianite princess. (25:14–18)

A new census. Now that the nation was camped by the Jordan River on the verge of entering the Promised Land, God commanded that a new census be taken of all men eligible to serve in the army, from age twenty and over. The Torah lists the tribes and their clans, and the total count was 601,730. (26:1–51)

The apportionment of the Promised Land. The Lord told Moses that the land will be apportioned to the tribes by lottery, and the size of each tribe's territory will be proportional to its population. (26:52–56)

The Levite census. The Torah lists the clans of the Levites. The Levites were not included in the total of the other Israelites; and the total of Levite males, from the age of one month and older, was 23,000. (26:57–65)

The daughters of Zelophehad. The five daughters of Zelophehad, of the tribe of Manasseh, approached Moses, Eleazar the High Priest, and the chieftains of the tribes, saying that their father, who was not a member of Korah's rebellion, died in the desert, and he had no sons. They requested to be given a plot of land within the territory of Manasseh, so that their father's name would not be lost from within the tribe. Moses asked the Lord what to answer, and the Lord said that whenever a man dies without sons, the man's property rights will be transferred to his daughters; and if there are no daughters either, the property rights will go to the man's brothers or to the closest relative. (27:1–11)

Moses appoints his successor. Even though Moses would not be allowed to enter the Promised Land, the Lord told Moses that he may see the land from a mountain across the river. Moses asked the Lord to appoint somebody who will lead the nation in battle when they enter the land. The Lord commanded Moses to select Joshua son of Nun and to invest him with some of Moses's authority. Moses did as the Lord commanded. (27:12–23)

Celebration of the festivals in the Tabernacle. The Lord spoke to Moses and told him that each day a burnt offering was to be brought in the morning and again at twilight. And the Torah lists the sacrifices that were to be brought on each of the festivals. (28:1 – 30:1)

Vows and oaths. If a man makes a vow or an oath to the Lord, he must fulfill his word. The same applies to a woman; except that, if she is a youth living in her father's house, her father may annul her vow or oath; or if she is a married woman, her husband may annul her vow or oath, on condition that the father or the husband does so immediately. (30:2–17)

War against the Midianites. Moses assembled the Israelite army, a thousand men from each of the twelve tribes, and attacked the Midianites in retaliation for what they had done to Israel (see 25:1–9). Israel defeated the Midianites and killed the five kings of Midian; and they also killed the prophet Balaam, by whose words the Midianite women had been sent to entice the Israelites. (Chapter 31)

The two and a half tribes. The tribes of Reuben and Gad had a lot of livestock, and they saw that the land Israel had conquered from Sihon and Og was excellent for grazing. So those two tribes came before Moses, Eleazar, and the tribal chieftains, and they requested to be given that land on the east side of the Jordan River as their inheritance, instead of land across the Jordan. After some discussion, it was agreed that those two tribes, and half the tribe of Manasseh, would get the territory of Sihon and Og. They may build cities there for their wives and children, and facilities for their livestock; but their men must remain with the Israelite army when they cross the Jordan, and they must remain with the army in combat until the conquest of the Promised Land is completed. (Chapter 32)

The route through the desert. The Torah lists the entire route of the Israelites from the time they departed Egypt until their arrival at the plains of Moab in the fortieth year. (Chapter 33)

The borders of the land of Canaan. The Lord told Moses the borders of the land to be apportioned by lot. In the south, the boundary extends from the wilderness of Zin on the border of Edom, from the eastern tip of the Dead Sea, to the brook of Egypt and the Mediterranean Sea. The western border is the Mediterranean Sea. In the north, the border extends from Mount Hor through the entrance of Hamath to Zedad, and southwards through Riblah and the eastern bank of Lake Kinnereth. The border then descends along the Jordan, through the Dead Sea. These were the borders for the nine and a half tribes within the land of Canaan. And the territory of Reuben, Gad, and half the tribe of Manasseh had already been apportioned across the Jordan River. (34:1–15)

The tribal chieftains. The Torah lists the names of the tribal chieftains who will lead the people of Israel into the land of Canaan. (34:16–29)

The Levite cities and the cities of refuge. Because the Levite population would be distributed among the twelve tribes and would not have any specified territory set aside for them, the Lord told Moses to tell the people of Israel to give the Levites 42 cities within the territory of the various tribes. In addition, the Levites will be given six cities—three across the Jordan and three within Canaan—that will be designated as cities of refuge, to which a person who committed accidental homicide could flee in order to escape the blood avenger. But asylum will be granted only for accidental homicide and not for murder. (Chapter 35)

The inheritance of the daughters of Zelophehad. The clan chieftains of the tribe of Manasseh questioned what would occur if Zelophehad's daughters were to marry men of other tribes. What would happen to their inherited land? At the Lord's direction, Moses answered that in that case, and in any case where a daughter inherits her father's land, the land will remain within the tribal territory of her father. The daughters of Zelophehad married their cousins, and their inherited land remained in the territory of Manasseh. (Chapter 36)

V. THE BOOK OF DEUTERONOMY
(*Devarim*)

Introduction to Moses's farewell address. In the fortieth year, as the Israelites were about to cross the Jordan River, Moses began his farewell to the nation, in which he reviewed some of the important events of the past forty years, and he expounded the principles of the laws that the Lord had given the nation during those years. (Deuteronomy 1:1–5)

Forty years in the desert. Moses recounted the episode of the spies, and how—because of the people's lack of trust that the Lord would enable them to possess the land He had promised them—the nation was condemned to spend forty years in the desert, until the generation of doubters passed away. But, Moses said, God also was angry at him, and God told Moses that he would not enter the Promised Land. Moses's narration then skips ahead to the Israelites' arrival at the border of Edom, the descendants of Esau. God did not allow Israel to attack Edom, and they took a circuitous route around Edom. Similarly, the Israelites were not permitted to war against Moab. But Israel did do battle against Sihon and Og, and they conquered the territory of those two kings (see Numbers 21:11 – 22:1). Og was the last surviving member of a race of giants who used to dwell there. And now, Moses, said, he instructed Joshua not to fear the Canaanites, because the Lord will give their land to the people of Israel. The Lord will do battle on behalf of Israel, and He will do to the Canaanites as He did to Sihon and Og. (1:1 – 3:22)

Moses's plea. Moses pleaded with God to allow him to cross the Jordan and to see the land that the Lord is giving to the Israelites. The Lord answered that Moses should not speak to Him any more about that matter. But God told Moses to go up the mountain, and he will see the land from across the river. (3:23–29)

Warnings. Moses warned Israel that they must not add to or subtract from what the Lord commanded. And when they enter the land, they must adhere to all of the Lord's teachings. They must always remember the awesome revelation at Mount Horeb, when God spoke the Decalogue to the assembled nation. They must remember it every day, and teach their children and grandchildren about it. But they must remember that they saw no image when the Lord spoke to them at Horeb. They must make no idols. Nor may they worship the sun, the moon, the stars, or any heavenly body. And they must not forget the covenant that the Lord made with them. Moses said that if, on taking possession of the land, Israel will worship idols and do evil, they will be exiled and scattered among the nations. But even then, if they seek the Lord with all their hearts, they will find Him. He will not abandon them, because He is a God of mercy, and He will not forget the covenant He made with the Patriarchs. They must know that the Lord is God in heaven above and on the earth below; there is no other beside Him. (4:1–40)

Three cities of refuge. Moses designated three cities to the east of the Jordan as cities of refuge: Bezer, Ramoth, and Golan. (4:41–49)

The Decalogue. Moses repeated the text of the Ten Commandments, with slight alteration in some of the phrasing. Also, the fourth Commandment here tells Israel to "Keep the Sabbath day," but—in contrast to the reason given in Exodus 20:11—the reason given here for the Sabbath is that God took the Israelites out of slavery in Egypt. (5:1 – 6:3)

The "Shma": "Listen, Israel: the Lord is our God; the Lord is one." The people of Israel must love their God with all their hearts. They must place these words in their hearts, teach them to their children, and recite them twice daily, morning and evening. They must bind them to their arms and between their eyes, and they must have them written on the doorposts of their dwellings. (6:4–9)

Remembering Egyptian bondage. Moses told the Israelites that when their children ask about the laws and the practices that the Lord commanded, they should tell their children that they were slaves in Egypt, and the Lord took the Israelites out of there, in order to give them the land that He had promised to their Patriarchs. And the Lord gave Israel laws and told them to revere Him, so that they will be righteous and meritorious before the Lord. (6:10–25)

The Canaanites. Moses reiterated God's warning not to make treaties with the Canaanites and not to intermarry with them. (7:1–11)

The Lord's blessings. Moses told the nation that if they follow the Lord's commandments, they will receive His blessings. They will possess the land and prosper, and they must not fear the Canaanites on account of their might and their numbers. They must remember what God did for Israel in Egypt and in the desert. The land they are about to enter is fertile and good. When they eat and are satiated, they should bless the Lord. (7:12 – 8:20)

The wickedness of the Canaanites, and the sins of Israel.

Moses told his nation that God will vanquish the Canaanites because of the their great wickedness, and because of His oath to the Patriarchs to give the land to them and their descendants. But the people of Israel must always remember how they angered God in the desert, and how their rebelliousness and their worship of the Golden Calf caused Moses to shatter the tablets. Then, when God was about to eradicate the Israelites and was about to annihilate Aaron because of his role in making the idol, Moses prayed to the Lord, and the Lord spared both Aaron and the nation. For they are His nation, which He brought out of Egypt with His great might and with an outstretched arm. (Chapter 9)

The second tablets, and the role of the Levites. Moses recounted how he had carved a new set of tablets, upon which God inscribed the Decalogue, and which Moses placed in the Ark. The Lord separated the Levites to bear the Ark of the Covenant, to serve the Lord, and to transmit the Lord's blessings to the people. Therefore, the Levites were given no territory as inheritance in the Promised Land. The Lord is their inheritance. (10:1–11)

Israel's duty in the land. Heaven and earth are the Lord's; and He chose the patriarchs of Israel, to give the land to their descendants. The people of Israel must purify their hearts and must not be rebellious. They must love the foreigner, "because you were foreigners in the land of Egypt." And they must do justice, because the Lord is a God of justice, Who shows no favoritism and Who upholds the rights of the downtrodden. Israel must keep the laws that the Lord commanded, so that they will prolong their days living in the land that the Lord is giving them, a land flowing with milk and honey, a land that is always under the Lord's watch. So long as Israel adheres to the Lord's commands, no nation will be able to stand against them, and all the territory from the desert to Lebanon, from the Euphrates River to the Mediterranean Sea, will be theirs. (10:12 – 11:25)

The place where the Lord's presence will dwell. When Israel is settled in the land, the Lord will designate a place where He will set His presence and where burnt offerings will be brought. Then, it will no longer be permitted to bring sacrifices anywhere else. Also, people will no longer be required to offer a sacrifice whenever they want to eat meat, as they were required to do in the desert. They will be allowed to slaughter animals for food anywhere, but they must slaughter according to the method that the Lord prescribed. (11:25 – 12:28)

Abolishing pagan cults. When Israel takes possession of the land, they must not be drawn into worship of Canaanite deities nor into adopting Canaanite modes of worship, because Canaanite rituals were loathsome to the Lord: they even offered their sons and daughters as sacrifices to their gods. Therefore, the sites of pagan rites must be destroyed. (12:1–3, & 12:29 – 13:1)

False prophets, and other temptations. If a prophet or a seer should arise among the Israelites and give a sign or a portent, but then tells people to worship an alien deity, the Israelites must not listen to him; and that false prophet must be put to death for his sedition. Also, if a relative or a friend entices you to worship of an alien deity, he too is guilty of sedition and incurs the death penalty. (13:2–19)

Children of the Lord. "You are children of the Lord your God." Do not cut yourselves nor shave the front of your heads in mourning for the dead, because you are a holy nation. The Torah now repeats the list of which animals the people of Israel are permitted to eat, and which are forbidden (compare Leviticus, Chapter 11), with a few additional permitted animals such as the deer, gazelle, and antelope. (14:1–21)

Tithes, loans, and charity. In certain years, a second tithe—one-tenth of a farmer's produce or of his firstborn livestock—must be brought to the appointed place that the Lord will designate, and eaten there. And the Levite must be given his due. If there is a poor person in need of a loan, do not hesitate to give him a loan; but it is forbidden to charge interest of another Israelite. And do not hesitate to give gifts to the destitute. Because on account of these acts, the Lord will bless you in all that you do. (14:22–15:11)

The Hebrew bondman. A Hebrew bondman is freed after six years. When he is released, you must give him generous gifts. But if he says he doesn't want to be liberated, you will pierce his ear with an awl, and he will remain your permanent bondman. (15:12–18)

The pilgrimage festivals. Every Israelite man is required to go to the place that the Lord will select, to celebrate each of the three pilgrimage festivals: Passover in the spring, *Shavuot*—the Feast of Weeks—seven weeks later, and *Sukkot*—the Feast of Huts—in the fall. (16:1–17)

Administration of justice. Judges and administrators must be appointed for every city. Do not pervert justice. Do not show favoritism, and do not accept a bribe. "Justice, justice shall you pursue." (16:18 – 17:7)

The High Court. If a case is too difficult for local judges to decide, whether it be a capital case, a criminal case, a tort, or a dispute between litigants, the case should be brought to the place that the Lord will choose. There, the authorities or the judges will render a verdict, and their verdict must be followed. (17:8–13)

Appointing a king. If the people of Israel say they want to appoint a king once they are settled in their land, they may do so. However, the Lord will choose the king. The king must not be a foreigner; nor may he have excessive horses, many wives, or excessive silver and gold. When he is seated on his throne, he must have a copy of the Torah written for him, and he must read from it every day of his life, so that he will be God-fearing and will learn to follow its laws, and so that he will not become haughty and consider himself above his brothers. (17:14–20)

Prophets. God warns the nation not to adopt the loathsome practices of the Canaanites. No Israelite may pass a son or daughter through fire. Sorcerers, mediums, and necromancers are forbidden. The Canaanites listen to sorcerers; but for Israel, God will appoint a prophet, an Israelite who, like Moses, will speak the word of God. (Chapter 18)

Three more cities of refuge. When the Israelites are settled in their land, they must designate three more cities of refuge within the land of Canaan. (19:1–15)

Witnesses in a criminal case. In a criminal case, the evidence may only be established by two or more witnesses. (19:16–21)

Preparing for war. When Israel is about to go to war against its enemies, the *kohen* should address the soldiers and exhort them not to fear their enemy, because the Lord will go with them. Any soldier who has betrothed a woman but not yet married her, he will be excused; and anybody who is excessively fearful of battle will also be excused. (20:1–9)

Waging war. When the army of Israel approaches an enemy city to wage war, they must first make an offer of peace. And if Israel besieges an enemy city, they must not cut down any fruit trees but may only cut down trees that bear no fruit to build siege-works. (20:10–20)

A woman captured in war. If an Israelite captures a woman in war and desires her, then, after she is given a thirty-day mourning period, he may marry her. But if he doesn't want to marry her, he must free her; he may not sell her as a slave. (21:10–14)

Inheritance. A firstborn son gets a larger inheritance than his siblings. If a man has two wives, and the oldest is the son of the wife he loves less, he must give the firstborn's inheritance to that son and not to the son of his preferred wife. (21:15–23)

Lost and found. If an Israelite finds another person's property, whether an animal or an object, he must return it to its owner. If he does not know who owns it, he must hold it until it is claimed, and then return it to the owner. (22:1–4)

Inappropriate garments. A woman may not wear a man's apparel; nor may a man wear a woman's dress. (22:5)

A protective fence. When building a house, there must be a fence on the roof, to prevent anybody from falling and getting killed. (22:8)

The *mamzer*. A *mamzer*—that is, the offspring of incest or adultery—may not marry an Israelite, nor may his descendants. (23:3)

Various prohibitions. An Ammonite or a Moabite man may not marry into the congregation of Israel. Israelites must not hate the Edomites, because the Edomites are brothers; nor may Israelites hate Egyptians, because the Israelites were foreigners in their land. There must not be either male or female harlots among the people of Israel. (Chapter 23)

Marriage and divorce. If a man marries a woman and later wants to divorce her, he must write her a divorce document and give it in her hand. (24:1–4)

Recent marriage. A man is exempt from military service for a year after marriage. (24:5–6)

Kidnapping. If someone abducts another and profits from the abduction, he shall be put to death. (24:7)

Leprosy. Remember that the Lord afflicted Miriam with leprosy (for speaking badly about her brother Moses). (24:8–9)

Laws of justice and charity. Parents must not die for their children's crimes, nor children for their parents' crimes. A person is punished only for his own crimes. When you harvest your field and forget a sheaf, do not go back; you must leave it for the needy. (24:10–22)

Levirate marriage. If a man has a married brother who dies childless, the surviving brother must take his brother's widow in levirate marriage, and the firstborn will be considered the deceased brother's. But if the surviving brother declines to marry her, they must perform a ceremony in which she removes his shoe and spits before him. (25:5–10)

Honesty in business. A merchant must have only honest weights and measures. (25:12–16)

Remembering the hatefulness of Amalek. Remember how Amalek attacked the Israelites when they were weak and weary and had just left Egypt. When the Israelites are in their land and are free of their enemies, they must erase the "memory" of Amalek. "Do not forget!" (25:17–19)

First fruits. When Israel is settled in its land, a farmer must bring his first fruits to the place the Lord will designate. There he will present his first fruits and thank the Lord for bringing the Israelites out of Egypt and for giving them the good land that He has given them. (Chapter 26)

Blessings and curses. The Lord commanded that when Israel enters the land, they should inscribe the words of the Torah on large rocks and place them on Mount Ebal. Moses selected six tribes to stand on that mountain, and the other six tribes to stand on the facing mountain, Mount Gerizim. The six tribes on Mount Gerizim will pronounce blessings to be given to Israel if the nation adheres to the Lord's commandments, and the other six will pronounce curses if Israel does not follow the Lord's commandments. If Israel follows His commandments, the land will be fertile, and the nation will live in prosperity and peace. But if Israel does not follow the commandments, then disease, pestilence, drought, famine, war, and exile will befall them. (Chapters 27–29)

The power of repentance. After Israel sins and is scattered among the nations, the people of Israel will contemplate the matter and take it to heart. When they return to the Lord, the Lord will return to them. He will gather them from the corners of the earth, and He will return the people of Israel to their land. And, Moses emphasized, repentance is not something distant, for which people must search; but it is within people's hearts to accomplish it. "Life and death I have set before you, blessing and curse. Choose life!" (Chapter 30)

Moses passes the torch. On God's direction, Moses appointed Joshua as his successor who was to lead the nation into the Promised Land. Moses wrote the Torah and gave it to the priests and the elders of Israel, telling them that in seven years, on the pilgrimage festival of *Sukkot*, they should assemble the people and read it to them. Also, the Lord taught Moses a poem and told him to write it down and to teach it to the people of Israel, so that it will stand as testimony and witness for them in their future tribulations. (Chapter 31)

The poetry of *Ha'azinu*. Moses calls heaven and earth to bear witness as he speaks God's words. The Lord chose Israel as His own, watching over them as an eagle over its young. He bore Israel on His wings, but they forsook him and sacrificed to other gods. They forgot the God Who made them, and the Lord will punish them for their sins. But in the end, when He sees that their strength has fled, He will avenge His people; He will wreak destruction on His foes—all those who have persecuted Israel. For He is the Lord, "and there is no god beside Me. I put to death and bring to life; I wound, and I will heal; and none can deliver from My hand." When Moses finished reciting the poem, he exhorted the people to be faithful to the Lord's teachings, so that they will endure in the land that God is giving them. Then the Lord commanded Moses to ascend Mount Nebo and look upon the Promised Land before he dies. (Chapter 32)

The blessings to the tribes of Israel. Moses gave an individual blessing to each of the tribes. (Chapter 33)

The death of Moses. Moses ascended Mount Nebo, facing Jericho. There, the Lord showed him the entire land that He was giving to the people of Israel. Moses died and was buried there; and nobody knows the site of his burial until this day. Joshua was filled with the spirit of wisdom, and the people followed him. Moses was 120 years old when he died, and the nation mourned him on the plains of Moab for thirty days. There has never arisen in Israel a prophet equal to Moses, to whom the Lord spoke face to face, and who performed the signs and the miracles that the Lord sent him to perform in the land of Egypt, "and all the mighty hand and all the awesome acts that Moses performed before the eyes of all of Israel." (Chapter 34)

THE PROPHETS

JOSHUA

The Lord speaks to Joshua. After the death of Moses, the Lord spoke to Joshua and told him to lead the people of Israel across the Jordan River into the land that the Lord is giving them, which will extend from the southern desert to Lebanon, and from the Euphrates River to the Mediterranean Sea. Just as the Lord was with Moses, so too He will be with Joshua. But, God said, Joshua must follow the dictates of the Torah and must study the Torah every day. (Joshua 1:1–9)

Joshua's initial orders. Joshua announced that in three days the nation would be crossing the Jordan, and the people should prepare. Then he addressed the tribes of Reuben, Gad, and half the tribe of Manasseh, saying they must remember their agreement with Moses. They should leave their wives, children, and livestock in the land that the Lord gave them across the Jordan, but the men must fight with the rest of the Israelite army until the entire land is conquered. They replied that they would comply with the agreement; and just as they obeyed Moses, they will obey Joshua. (1:10–18)

Joshua dispatches spies to Jericho. Joshua secretly sent two spies to Jericho. Arriving in Jericho, the spies lodged at the house of a woman named Rahab, who ran an inn and a brothel there. The king of Jericho was told about Israelite spies who had come during the night, and he demanded that Rahab turn them over.

But Rahab had hidden the spies on her roof under stalks of flax. She told the king's messengers that two strangers had come to her inn, and she didn't know from where they had come. But, she said, they had left just as the city gate was closing for the night. So the king's men chased after them, and they closed the city gate behind them. Rahab then went up to the roof and told Joshua's spies that she knows their God is the true God in heaven above and in the earth below. She said that she knows of the miracles that God performed for Israel, and that He will give the land to them. She will help the spies escape, but they must swear that when the Israelite army conquers the city, they will spare her family. The spies swore. Her inn was in the city wall, and she lowered them out a window by a crimson cord. She told them to head for the hills and remain there for three days, until the king's men return. The spies instructed her to leave the crimson cord hanging out the window and to gather all her family at her house. The Israelite soldiers will know not to attack that house. The spies stayed in the hills for three days and returned to camp. They reported to Joshua son of Nun that the city is theirs, and the spirit of its people has melted away. (Chapter 2)

Crossing the Jordan. Early the next morning, Joshua and the people of Israel marched to the Jordan River, and they camped there for three days. At Joshua's direction, the priests took up the Ark of the Covenant, and the people followed them. When the priests' feet touched the water, the water flowing from upstream stood like a wall, so that the water flowing downstream from them left the riverbed dry. The priests carrying the Ark stood in the middle of the riverbed until the entire nation had crossed the Jordan on dry land. (Chapter 3)

Commemorating the crossing. On God's command, Joshua selected one man from each of the twelve tribes and told them to pick twelve rocks from the middle of the Jordan riverbed and carry the rocks on their shoulders. When the entire nation had crossed, the priests carrying the Ark of the Covenant moved out of the riverbed to the front of the people, and the upstream waters of the Jordan resumed their course. That day, the Lord elevated Joshua's status in the eyes of the people, and they revered him as they had revered Moses. The nation camped for the night at Gilgal, to the east of Jericho; and there Joshua had the twelve rocks set up to commemorate the crossing, so that all will remember how the Lord dried up the Jordan just as He had dried the seabed after the Exodus from Egypt. And when all the Amorite kings west of the Jordan and all the kings of the Canaanites by the sea heard that the Lord had dried up the Jordan for the Israelites, they lost heart. (4:1–5:1)

Gilgal. Israelites born during the forty years in the desert had not been circumcised; so now, Joshua had the people make flint knives, and he had all uncircumcised Israelite males circumcised. They remained at Gilgal until all had recovered, and there they celebrated the Passover festival. On the following morning, when they ate the produce of the land, the Manna stopped. (5:2–12)

The attack against Jericho. Joshua looked up and saw a man standing with drawn sword. Joshua approach and asked, "Are you one of ours, or of our enemies?" The man replied, "I am captain of the Lord's army. I have come!" On the angel's instructions, Joshua had the priests take the Ark of the Covenant and march around the walls of Jericho each day for six days. Seven priests went before the Ark, blowing rams' horns as they marched. Before them marched the vanguard, and the rear guard marched behind. And on the seventh day, they circled the walls seven times, with the priests blowing the horns as they marched. Upon completing the seventh circuit of the city, Joshua commanded everyone to shout. The people gave a mighty shout, and the entire wall collapsed. Joshua ordered his army to advance, but he cautioned his people to take no booty, on pain of death; the silver, gold, copper, and iron objects in the city would be reserved for the Lord's treasury. The Hebrew army entered the city, and Joshua assigned the two spies to rescue Rahab and her family. The Israelites burned the city to the ground; but Rahab and her family were spared, with all their possessions; and she remained with Israel. Then Joshua pronounced a curse on anybody who will rebuild Jericho. (5:13 – 6:27)

The battle of Ai. Joshua sent spies to the Amorite city of Ai, which was east of Bethel. In accordance with the spies' recommendation, Joshua sent only about 3,000 men to attack the city; but the men of Ai came out in force, and the Israelite troops fled before them. Joshua cried out to the Lord, and the Lord answered that Israel had sinned: the ban on taking booty in Jericho had been violated. When the perpetrator was discovered and executed for his crime, the Lord told Joshua to lead his army against Ai, and now he would prevail. Joshua split his army into three divisions: the main force to the north in front of the city's gate, a smaller force to the west, and a large one hidden behind the city. The Amorite army came out to engage the Israelites, and again the Israelite army fled, leading the men of Ai far from their city. The large Israelite force hidden behind the city rushed forward, overwhelmed the city, and set it on fire. Then, the main Israelite force turned around, and the Amorite army was trapped between them and the other Israelites emerging from the burning city. None escaped. Joshua had the king of Ai executed, and the king's corpse was buried at the city gate. (7:1 – 8:29)

Reading the blessings and the curses. Joshua built an altar and inscribed the words of the Torah on large rocks on Mount Ebal, as Moses had commanded. Joshua had half the tribes stand facing Mount Gerizim and half facing Mount Ebal, as Moses had prescribed. (See Deuteronomy, Chapter 27.) And Joshua read to them all the blessings and curses that Moses had written in the Torah. (8:30–35)

The Gibeonites. The inhabitants of Gibeon sent men to Joshua's camp in Gilgal to make a treaty with their city. The Israelites were not allowed to make treaties with any cities within the land of Canaan, and therefore the Gibeonite emissaries pretended to be aliens who had come from afar. Thus, they tricked Joshua into making a treaty. But three days later, it was discovered that their city was nearby. When Joshua confronted the elders of Gibeon regarding their deceit, they answered that they had feared for their lives. Joshua said that Israel would honor its treaty with Gibeon, but henceforth the Gibeonites will forever serve Israel as woodcutters and water-bearers. (Chapter 9)

The attack of the five kings. When the Amorite king of Jerusalem heard about the defeat of Ai and about the Gibeonites' treaty with Israel, he assembled the kings of four other Amorite cities, and together they attacked Gibeon. The Gibeonites requested Joshua's assistance, and Joshua immediately mobilized his army and marched all night to engage the combined armies of the five Amorite kings. He took the five kings by surprise and inflicted on them a crushing defeat. As the Amorite armies were fleeing, Joshua commanded the sun and the moon to stand still so the battle could continue. And great stones fell from the sky, killing many of the fleeing Amorites. During the battle, the five kings escaped, and they hid in a cave. But the Israelites discovered them there. After defeating the Amorite armies, Joshua had the kings executed and their bodies hung on trees. In the evening, their corpses were thrown into the cave, and the cave was sealed. And after vanquishing those five kings, Joshua conquered numerous other kings encompassing the entirety of southern Canaan, up to Gaza. (10:1–28)

Conquering the land. After Joshua conquered seven additional cities, the king of Hazor assembled a coalition of armies of the Canaanites, Amorites, Hittites, Jebusites, Perizzites, and Hivvites from cities throughout Canaan. The coalition fielded a huge fighting force of infantry, horses, and chariots, and they camped by the waters of Merom to do battle with Israel. But the Lord told Joshua not to fear them. Joshua launched a surprise attack, winning a decisive victory against them. After defeating the coalition, Joshua conquered cities throughout the land of Canaan, from the desert in the south up to Lebanon in the north, and from the Jordan River and the Dead Sea in the east to Gaza in the west, a total of 31 cities. And he wiped out the giants who lived in the hill country and in all the land of Israel, except that some remained in the Philistine cities. Thus, Israel conquered the bulk of the land of Canaan; but after many years, the five cities of the Philistines and pockets of Canaanite territory along the Mediterranean coast and southern Lebanon had not yet been conquered. (Chapters 11, 12, & 13)

Apportioning the land. Moses had previously assigned the land across the Jordan River to the tribes of Reuben and Gad, and half the tribe of Manasseh. Now, the land of Canaan west of the Jordan was apportioned by lot among the remaining nine and a half tribes. The portion of Judah was farthest south, bordering on Edom. Caleb, of the tribe of Judah, was given the city of Hebron as reward for his role in countering the unfavorable report about Canaan that the spies had given 45 years earlier. The men of Judah conquered all the cities within their assigned territory, but they did not displace the Jebusite inhabitants of Jerusalem, and they lived among the Jebusites there. (Chapters 14–17)

The Tabernacle, the cities of refuge, and the Levite cities. When the entire land of Canaan came under Israelite control, the Tabernacle was set up in Shiloh, and a meeting of all the tribes was held there. Then the Lord spoke to Joshua and told him to designate three cities of refuge in the land of Canaan, in addition to the three that Moses had designated across the Jordan River. So Joshua set aside Kedesh, Shechem, and Hebron as cities of refuge for those who committed accidental homicide. And the Levites, who did not have their own region, had cities allotted to them throughout the land. (Chapters 18–21)

The tribes across the Jordan River. Joshua summoned the tribes of Reuben, Gad, and the half-tribe of Manasseh and told them that they had fulfilled their obligation of serving in the army and could now return to their families in their land to the east of the Jordan. Soon after, they built an altar there. When the other tribes heard of this, they were incensed: they regarded the building of an altar across the river as a rebellion against the Lord and a denial of the authority of the Tabernacle in Shiloh. So Joshua sent Phineas the priest and ten clan chieftains to the two and a half tribes across the Jordan. The tribes across the river replied that they had not intended their altar to be a rebellion, nor would they bring sacrifices upon it. That altar was to be a symbol and a witness of the bond between them and the tribes to the west of the Jordan. Their explanation was accepted, and the altar was named "Witness." (Chapter 22)

The last days of Joshua. When Joshua was very old, he assembled the tribes of Israel at Shechem, and he exhorted them to continue serving the Lord. They must not intermarry with the Canaanites who were still in their midst, and they must not adopt the worship of Canaanite gods. The Lord has given the land of Canaan to the people of Israel; but, Joshua cautioned, if Israel deviates from the Lord's teachings and merges with the remaining Canaanites or adopts their practices, Israel will be punished and will be exiled from the land. The people responded that they will serve the Lord alone. Joshua died at the age of 110 years, and he was buried on his property. And the body of Joseph that Moses had brought out of Egypt was buried in the city of Shechem, in the land that Joseph's father Jacob had purchased from Hamor the father of Shechem. (Chapters 23 & 24)

JUDGES

The conquest of Bezek. After the death of Joshua, the tribes of Judah and Simeon defeated an army of 10,000 at Bezek, and they captured Adoni-Bezek, king of Bezek. They cut off his thumbs and big toes, and he said, "As I have done, so God has done to me," because he used to have seventy kings whom he had conquered, with their thumbs and big toes cut off, picking at scraps under his table. (Judges 1:1–7)

Jerusalem. The army of Judah conquered Jerusalem and set it on fire. The Israelite tribes conquered many cities, but they often did not dispossess the Canaanites in those cities, and the Canaanites continued to live among them. (1:8–36)

The remaining Canaanites and Philistines. When Joshua and all of his generation had died, the next generation, who had not experienced the great wonders that God had performed for Israel, began to worship the gods of the Canaanites. The Philistines and some of the Canaanites remained unconquered, and their presence served as a test of Israel's faithfulness to the Lord. (2:1 – 3:4)

Othniel, the first of the Judges. The Israelites intermarried with the Canaanites, Hittites, Amorites, and other locals, and they worshipped their gods. As punishment, the Lord delivered Israel into the hands of Cushan-Rishatayim, the king of Aram, who ruled over them for eight years. The people cried out to the Lord, and the Lord appointed as their redeemer Caleb's kinsman

Othniel, who during Joshua's lifetime had been the conqueror of Hebron. The spirit of the Lord filled Othniel, and he defeated Cushan-Rishatayim's army. And the land remained at peace for forty years. (3:5–11)

Ehud. After the death of Othniel, Israel sinned again, and the Lord again allowed Israel to fall into the hands of their enemies. Eglon, the king of Moab, assembled an army of Moabites, Ammonites, and Amalekites. He defeated Israel, and the Israelites became his subjects for eighteen years. The Israelites cried out to the Lord, and the Lord appointed Ehud son of Gera to redeem them. Ehud was sent to Moab to bring Israel's tribute to the king. Ehud, who was left-handed, hid a two-edged dagger under his cloak, and he went before the king, who was a very fat man. After presenting Israel's tribute, he told the king that he had a secret message, and the king dismissed his men. Ehud said his message was from God, and Eglon immediately rose from his throne. Ehud quickly drew his dagger and plunged it into Eglon's belly. He then locked the doors and escaped. On returning to Israel, he led the Israelite army to victory over Moab. (3:15–30)

Shamgar. After Ehud came Shamgar son of Anath, who fought against the Philistines and slew 600 of them. (3:31)

Deborah and Barak. Jabin, the Canaanite king of Hazor, subjugated and oppressed Israel for 25 years; and his general, Sisra, commanded an army of 900 iron chariots. Deborah the prophetess, who was the leader of Israel at that time, summoned Barak son of Avinoam, who was commander of the Israelite army, and ordered him in the Lord's name to take 10,000 troops and attack Sisra. Barak answered that he would do so only if Deborah would go with him. Deborah consented to go with him; but, she told Barak, the glory of conquest will not be his: Sisra will be delivered into the hands of a woman. Barak mustered his troops on Mount Tabor, and they charged down the mountain against Sisra's chariots. Sisra's army panicked, and all were slain. Sisra fled on foot, and he sought refuge in the tent of Heber the Kenite, who was supposedly an ally of Hazor. But while Sisra was asleep, Heber's wife Yael killed him by driving a tent pin through his head. (Chapter 4)

Victory. After the defeat of Jabin, Deborah and Barak sang a song of victory. (Chapter 5)

Gideon. Israel again sinned against the Lord, and the Lord delivered them into the hands of Midian. For seven years, the Midianites ravaged Israel's crops, and food became scarce. An angel of the Lord came to Gideon, the youngest son of a family in the land of Manasseh, who was beating wheat inside a winepress in order to be hidden from the Midianites. The angel said, "The Lord is with you, brave warrior!" And the angel appointed Gideon as the Lord's messenger to deliver Israel from the Midianites. But Gideon asked for a sign that it was indeed an angel. Gideon brought an offering to the Lord and placed it on a rock. The angel touched the offering with his staff, and flames rose from the rock, consuming the offering. Then Gideon knew that it was indeed an angel who had spoken to him. That night, the Lord spoke to Gideon and told him to destroy the altar to the pagan god Baal on his father's land, and to erect an altar to God. But Gideon was afraid to do it by day, because he feared that people would stop him. So, with the help of ten of his father's slaves, he demolished the altar during the night. In the morning, when the townspeople found out that it was Gideon's doing, they sought to kill him. But Gideon's father said about Baal, "If he is a god, let him fight his own battles." From that day onward, they called Gideon "Jerubaal," meaning "Let Baal fight him." (6:1–32)

Gideon's battle against the Midianites. The Midianites, Amalekites, and people of the east joined forces and assembled in the Valley of Jezreel. Gideon enlisted troops numbering 32,000, but God told him there were too many. Therefore, at God's direction, Gideon selected 300 soldiers to fight the enemy. Gideon divided his 300 men into three squadrons, and he gave each man a ram's horn and a jar containing a torch. Late at night, he and his men surrounded the enemy camp. They sounded their horns, smashed the jars, and shouted loudly. The Midianites and their allies thought they were being attacked by a large force, and they fled into the hills. Gideon sent word to the Israelites in the hill country, and they pursued and killed the fleeing enemy. And the two Midianite generals were captured and executed. (6:33 – 7:25)

The two kings of Midian. Although the Midianite generals were captured, the two kings of Midian escaped, and Gideon's men pursued them across the Jordan River. When the two kings were captured and executed, the people of Israel asked Gideon to rule over them; and after Gideon, they said, his son and grandson would continue to rule over Israel. But Gideon refused, saying that neither he nor his son would rule over them. (Chapter 8)

Abimelekh, son of Gideon. After Gideon's death, Abimelekh, one of Gideon's sons by a maidservant, with the support of the citizens of Shechem, declared himself king. He killed his seventy brothers, and only Yotham, Gideon's youngest son, survived. Yotham cursed both Abimelekh and the citizens of Shechem. After a reign of three years, the people of Shechem rebelled against Abimelekh.

Abimelekh's men massacred the rebels, but Abimelekh was killed. Yotham's curse was fulfilled. (Chapter 9)

Tola son of Pua, and Jair of Gilead. The next two judges were Tola, who led Israel for 23 years, and Jair, who led Israel for 22 years. After their deaths, Israel again went astray, and they worshipped Baal and the gods of the surrounding nations. And God allowed the Philistines and the Ammonites to subjugate Israel and oppress them. At first, Ammon crushed the Israelites who lived across the Jordan. Then the Ammonites crossed the river to make war against the other tribes of Israel, and they camped in Gilead. The people declared that whoever would lead them in battle against Ammon would become the chieftain of all Gilead. (Chapter 10)

Jephthah. Jephthah the Gileadite, who was the despised son of a prostitute, was a mighty warrior; and he became general of Israel. He sent a message to the Ammonite king, offering peace. The Ammonite king replied that when Israel came out of Egypt, they seized the land across the Jordan; and the king demanded as a condition for peace that Israel cede to him all their land across the Jordan. Jephthah replied that Israel had not seized the land, but that the two Amorite kings, Sihon and Og, had attacked Israel, and the Israelites had defeated them in battle. The king of Ammon did not accept Jephthah's offer of peace, and Jephthah defeated the Ammonites in battle. But when Jephthah returned, he sacrificed his daughter in fulfillment of a vow he had made before the battle. (Chapter 11)

The complaint of Ephraim. The men of Ephraim complained that Jephthah had not called them to fight with him against the Ammonites, and they threatened to burn Jephthah's house down. Jephthah answered that he had called them, but they didn't come.

The Ephraimites were not placated, and a battle ensued. Jephthah's army defeated the men of Ephraim. (12:1–7)

Ivzan, Elon, and Avdon. After Jephthah, the judges who led Israel were Ivzan of Bethlehem, who was followed by Elon the Zebulonite, followed by Avdon son of Hillel. (12:8–15)

Manoah and his wife. The people of Israel again sinned against the Lord, and the Philistines subjugated them. At that time, there was a man named Manoah of the tribe of Dan, and his wife was barren. An angel appeared to her and told her that she will become pregnant and bear a son who will deliver Israel from the Philistines. But the child must be a nazirite from the time of conception: he must have no wine or beer, and he must not cut his hair. She told Manoah what "the man of God" had said to her, adding that his appearance was awe-inspiring, "like an angel." Manoah prayed to God to send the man back, to give them more instructions. The angel later returned to Manoah's wife when she was alone in the field, and she called her husband. The angel reiterated that Manoah's wife must not drink wine or beer, or consume any product of grapes, and they must be careful that the child not be in contact with any ritual defilement. Manoah sacrificed a young goat to the Lord, and, as the fire ascended from the altar, the angel went up to heaven in the flame. Only then did Manoah realize that it was an angel who had spoken to them. The child was born, and his mother named him Samson. Samson grew up, and the Lord blessed him. (Chapter 13)

Samson and the Philistines. Samson went to Timnah, and there he saw a Philistine woman whom he desired. His parents objected to his marrying a Philistine, but they didn't know that it was God's will; and Samson persisted. On the way to Timnah, a lion attacked

Samson, and he tore the lion apart with his bare hands. Months later, when he returned to Timnah for the wedding, Samson saw there was a beehive in the lion's carcass, with honey. At the wedding feast, Samson posed a riddle to thirty of the Philistine men: "From the eater came something to eat, and from the mighty came sweetness." If they solve the riddle, Samson will owe them thirty suits of clothing; and otherwise, they will owe him. When they couldn't solve the riddle, they threatened Samson's bride, saying they will burn down her father's house if she doesn't extract the answer from Samson. She nagged him each day; and on the seventh day, he told her. When the Philistines solved the riddle and Samson realized how they knew, the Lord's spirit came over him, and he went to the Philistine city of Ashkelon. There he killed thirty of its men, and he took their clothes to give to the men of Timnah. He returned to his father's house in a rage. (Chapter 14)

Samson's return. After some time had passed, Samson returned to visit his wife, and he brought a present. But her father refused to admit him, saying he had thought Samson now hated her, so he had given her in marriage to one of the guests who had attended her wedding to Samson. He offered Samson her younger sister, who, he said, was even more beautiful. But Samson warned that now he will not be culpable for the harm that he will inflict. Samson went out and caught three hundred foxes. He tied their tails together and placed a torch between each pair of tails. He lit the torches and released the foxes among the Philistines' wheat; and the Philistines' grain, vineyards, and olive trees were set afire. (14:20 – 15:5)

The jawbone of an ass. When the Philistines learned who had burned their fields, they set Samson's wife and her father on fire.

Samson retaliated, killing many Philistines, and he went to dwell in a crevice among the rocks in the land of Judah. The Philistines sent troops into Judah to arrest Samson, and they demanded that the Judeans deliver Samson to them. The Judeans sent 3,000 men to arrest Samson, and he agreed to be bound with ropes if the Judeans agreed not to harm him. When Samson reached the Philistine camp, the Lord's spirit enveloped him, and he easily ripped his ropes off. He came upon the jawbone of an ass, and with it he killed a thousand Philistines. Samson led Israel for twenty years. (15:6–20)

Samson in Gaza. Samson went to the Philistine city of Gaza, and there he lay with a prostitute. The men of Gaza set up an ambush at the city gate, expecting to attack him at daybreak. But Samson arose at midnight, ripped out the gate and the gateposts, and carried them away on his shoulders. (16:1–3)

Delilah. Samson fell in love with a Philistine woman named Delilah. The Philistine lords came to her and told her to seduce Samson and find out wherein lies his great strength and how they may overpower him; and each of them will reward her with 1,100 shekels of silver. Delilah nagged Samson for many days, until he told her he was a nazirite from the time he was in his mother's womb, and if his hair were cut, he would become no stronger than an ordinary man. Delilah called the Philistine lords to come, and they brought the promised money with them. She put Samson to sleep on her lap, and she cut his hair. Then she called out, "The Philistines are upon you!" Samson awoke and tried to break his bonds, but the Lord's spirit had left him, and he could not free himself. The Philistines took hold of him, and they gouged out his eyes. They took him to Gaza and put him in bronze shackles; and he became a mill-slave. But during his captivity, his hair began to grow back. (16:4–22)

The feast of Dagon. The lords of the Philistines assembled in a temple for a great celebration to honor their god Dagon. They brought Samson from prison and made him dance before them. They then put him between two of the pillars that held up the temple. Samson prayed to God to give him strength just one more time. He cried out, "Let me die with the Philistines," as he pulled on the two pillars and brought the ceiling crashing down, killing Samson and all the Philistine chieftains. (16:23–31)

Civil war. In those days, there was as yet no king in Israel, and there was much lawlessness. There was a certain Levite living in the hill country of Ephraim, and he had a concubine from Bethlehem in the land of Judah. The concubine left the Levite and returned to her father in Bethlehem. After four months, her husband went to Bethlehem and convinced her to return with him. On the way, they stopped at Gibeah in the territory of Benjamin, where an old man invited them into his house. But soon after they had eaten, the townsfolk came pounding on his door and forced the old man to give them the Levite's concubine. The townsfolk raped her all night. At dawn she returned to the old man's house and collapsed outside; and when her husband arose and opened the door, he found his concubine lying dead. He cut up her body into twelve parts and sent the parts to each of the tribes of Israel. The husband explained what the men of Gibeah had done, and he demanded action to punish the people of Gibeah. All the tribes were horrified, and they conscripted a large army. They demanded that the tribe of Benjamin hand over the perpetrators of the crime, but the Benjaminites refused.

A civil war ensued, during which most of the Benjaminites were killed, and their cities were burnt to the ground. Only 600 men of Benjamin survived, and they fled to the desert, where they hid for four months. (Chapters 17–20)

Peace is restored. After the war ended, the victors realized they could not allow one of the tribes of Israel to disappear, and they made peace with the remnant of Benjamin. But there were no women remaining in Benjamin, and the other tribes had all taken an oath not to give their daughters in marriage to any men of Benjamin. On inquiry, it was found that one town had failed to send soldiers for the Israelite army, and they had not participated in the oath. As punishment for their failure to comply with the draft, a contingent of the Israelite army was sent to that town with orders to kill all the townsmen and their wives. The maidens of the town were spared, and they were sent to the men of Benjamin for them to marry. Thus, the tribe of Benjamin was restored to life, and they rebuilt their cities. But still, there was no king in Israel, and everybody did as he pleased. (Chapter 21)

THE FIRST BOOK OF SAMUEL

The birth of the prophet Samuel. Hannah, a childless woman, went to the Tabernacle in Shiloh to pray for a child. Eli the priest blessed her and told her that God will answer her prayer. She promised God that if He gives her a son, she will dedicate that son to God's service. Indeed, she gave birth to a son, and she called her son Samuel, meaning "I asked the Lord for him." When the child was weaned, she returned to Shiloh with the child. She prayed a long prayer, and she left Samuel in the Tabernacle, for Eli the priest to train him in the service of the Lord. Hannah and her husband Elkanah visited Samuel at the Tabernacle when they brought their annual sacrifice, and Eli blessed them to have more children. Hannah bore three sons and two daughters. (1 Samuel 1:1 – 2:21)

Eli's sons. Eli the priest was very old, and Eli's sons Hofni and Pinehas were scoundrels. When people brought sacrifices to the Tabernacle, Eli's sons threatened them with violence and extorted from them portions of the meat for themselves. And they lay with wanton women at the entrance of the Tabernacle. Eli gently asked his sons to stop, but they continued in their evil ways. A man of God told Eli that the Lord had intended for Eli and his family to remain in His service forever. But, the man said, since the Lord has been dishonored, after Eli, the Lord will appoint another priest who will be faithful to Him. And Eli's sons will both die on the same day. (2:12–17 & 2:22–36)

The Lord reveals himself to Samuel. In the Tabernacle one night, while Samuel was still a child, the Lord called to him. Samuel thought it was Eli who had called him; but, after the call repeated itself twice more, Eli realized that it was the Lord who was calling, and he told Samuel that when the Lord calls to him again, he should answer that he is ready to receive God's message. Samuel did so, and the Lord told Samuel that He will fulfill the punishment that the man of God had told Eli, on account of Eli's sons' sacrilege and evil. In the morning, Samuel was afraid to tell Eli what the Lord had said, but Eli insisted. Samuel told him all, and Eli accepted God's judgement. Samuel grew up, and the Lord was with him. And all of Israel trusted him as a true prophet of the Lord. (Chapter 3)

Israel battles the Philistines. Israel engaged the Philistines in battle. Four thousand Israelites were killed, and Israel's army was routed. The elders of Israel sent men to Shiloh and brought the Ark of the Covenant to the Israelite camp. When the Philistines heard that the Ark of the Covenant had come, they were afraid, because of what God had done to the Egyptians. But in the ensuing battle, the Philistines overwhelmed the army of Israel and captured the Ark of the Covenant. When Eli heard about Israel's defeat, and that both of his sons had been killed and the Ark of the Covenant captured, he fell backwards and broke his neck. His daughter-in-law, the wife of Pinehas, went into labor and died in childbirth. As she was dying, she named her son Ichabod—"without Glory"—because, she said, with the Ark's capture, the Glory of God had departed. (Chapter 4)

The temple of Dagon. The Philistines took the Ark of the Covenant to the Philistine city of Ashdod and placed it in the temple of their god Dagon. The next morning, they found Dagon's statue lying face-down before the Ark. They righted the idol, but on the following morning they found it lying on the ground, with its severed head and hands lying on the threshold of the temple. And God punished all the people of Ashdod and its suburbs with hemorrhoids. The Philistines decided to send the Ark to the city of Gath; but there also, everyone was stricken with hemorrhoids. They then sent the Ark to Ekron. There, many people died, and the fear of death was upon the remaining populace. (Chapter 5)

The return of the Ark. After seven months, the land was ravaged by mice, and the Philistines feared that God would punish them as He had punished Egypt. They decided they must send the Ark back, with payment of an indemnity. So they made five golden hemorrhoids and five golden mice, corresponding to the five Philistine cities, and they placed those objects together with the Ark on a cart pulled by a pair of cows. They let the cows pull the cart wherever they pleased, and the cows took the cart directly to Beth-Shemesh. (Chapter 6)

Samuel exhorts the nation to return to the Lord. The Ark was taken to the town of Kiriath-Yearim, and there it remained for twenty years. Samuel assembled all of Israel at Mizpah. He exhorted the nation to return to the Lord with all their hearts and to abandon their worship of alien gods. The people listened to him, and Samuel re-consecrated the nation. The lords of the Philistines heard of the great assembly, and the Philistine army advanced against Mizpah. Samuel then brought a burnt offering and prayed to the Lord, whereupon there was a terrifying thunderstorm. The army of Israel pursued the Philistines, defeated them, and recaptured all the territory that the Philistines had taken from Israel. (Chapter 7)

The people want a king. When Samuel was old, he appointed his two sons as judges over Israel. But his sons were dishonest, and the people rejected their leadership. They asked Samuel to appoint a king to rule over them. Samuel was opposed to Israel's having a king, but the Lord told him to yield to the people's request. (Chapter 8)

Saul. Saul, son of Kish of the tribe of Benjamin, was a very tall man. One day, Saul went searching for some of his father's donkeys that had gone astray. When the hour was late, Saul's servant suggested that they stop at a nearby town where there was a man of God. Samuel encountered Saul in the street, and God informed Samuel that this was the man whom He has chosen to be king. Saul asked Samuel directions to the seer's house. Samuel identified himself as the seer, and he invited Saul and his servant to a feast. To Saul's confusion, Samuel seated him at the head of the table and gave him the choicest cut of meat. When the feast was over, Samuel poured oil on Saul's head and, in God's name, anointed him ruler over Israel. Saul had gone in search of donkeys; but instead of donkeys, he found kingship. (9:1 – 10:1)

Saul's return home. Samuel told Saul to go to Gilgal and wait for him there. But, Samuel told him, on the way he will meet a group of prophets. The divine spirit will envelop Saul, he will prophesy with them, and he will be a changed man. And so it was. When Saul got home and told about his meeting with Samuel, Saul's uncle asked about what Samuel had said. Saul replied that Samuel told him the donkeys had been found. But Saul said nothing about being anointed king. (10:2–16)

Saul's public coronation. Samuel summoned the nation to Mizpah. But when he presented the people with God's choice of ruler, Saul could not be found. He was hiding. God told Samuel where Saul was; and when Samuel presented him to the people, he was a head taller than everybody else. The people acclaimed him, shouting "Long live the king!" Samuel then explained to the people the laws pertaining to the king, and he wrote the laws in a book. Saul went home to Gibeah, and there, some miscreants mocked him. But he kept silent. (10:17–27)

War with the Ammonites. Nahash, king of Ammon, besieged the Israelite town of Jabesh-Gilead. The inhabitants of Jabesh sued for peace, but Nahash demanded that, as a condition of their surrender, the right eye of every inhabitant be gouged out. The elders of Jabesh requested seven days to consider, and they sent messengers throughout Israel requesting assistance. When the messengers came to Saul, the spirit of God enveloped him. He assembled an army of 300,000 and attacked the Ammonites, winning a great victory. The people asked Samuel to bring forth those who had rejected Saul's kingship and have them executed. But Saul refused to mar the victory celebration with an execution. And Samuel called the nation again to Gilgal, where he re-inaugurated Saul as king of Israel. (Chapter 11)

Samuel warns the nation. Samuel warned that God will be with His nation if both they and their king adhere to God's laws; but if they do not, then they and their king will be punished. Nevertheless, God will not abandon His people. (Chapter 12)

Rebellion against Philistine domination. King Saul kept an army of 3,000 men: 2,000 under his command, and 1,000 under his son Jonathan; and he sent the rest of his troops home. Jonathan led his men against the Philistines and killed the local Philistine official. The Philistines were infuriated, and they assembled a large force to attack Israel. While Saul awaited Samuel's arrival, many of Saul's soldiers deserted. Saul, unable to stop the desertions, performed the ritual sacrifice that Samuel was supposed to perform. And just as he finished doing so, Samuel arrived and reprimanded Saul. (13:1–14)

Jonathan attacks the Philistines. As the Philistines began to advance against the Israelites, just 600 men remained to King Saul, armed only with axes and sharpened farm tools. There were no smiths in Israel, because the Philistines wanted the Hebrews to be unable to make swords or spears. Only Saul and Jonathan had swords. Jonathan sneaked out of camp with his arms-bearer and raided the Philistine camp, killing twenty men. Terror broke out among the Philistines, and an earthquake occurred, further heightening the Philistines' terror. Saul pursued the fleeing Philistines and commanded, on pain of death, that no man shall eat that day until the battle was done. Jonathan, who had not heard Saul's command, found some wild honey and took a taste. When Saul heard that Jonathan had eaten, he wanted to execute Jonathan, but the people declared Jonathan a hero, and thus they saved him from Saul's wrath. (13:15 – 14:46)

Saul's wars against Israel's enemies. Once Saul had secured his kingship, he waged war against all of Israel's enemies, including Moabites, Ammonites, and Edomites, and he defeated them. And war against the Philistines continued throughout his reign. (14:47–52)

Saul's war against Amalek. Samuel told Saul that the Lord commanded him to attack Amalek, Israel's long-time enemy. He was to spare nobody, take no prisoners, take no booty, and kill the Amalekite king Agag. Saul's army defeated the Amalekites; but Saul, out of fear of his men, allowed his army to take booty, and he spared the life of Agag. The Lord told Samuel that Saul had disobeyed God's command and was no longer fit to be king of Israel. Samuel was very distressed, and he pleaded with God all night, to no avail. In the morning, Samuel went to Saul and told him that because he had failed to follow God's command, and because he had failed to show leadership, the Lord has rejected him as king. When Samuel turned to leave, Saul seized the fringe of Samuel's coat, and the coat ripped. Samuel turned to Saul and said, "The Lord has this day ripped the kingship of Israel away from you and has given it to one more worthy than you." Samuel then took a sword and executed the Amalekite king. (Chapter 15)

Appointing a new king. The Lord told Samuel to stop mourning Saul's being deposed, and He commanded Samuel to go to the town of Bethlehem to appoint a new king. There, at the Lord's instruction, Samuel went to the home of Jesse and anointed Jesse's seventh and youngest son David, a shepherd, as king of Israel. (16:1–13)

David the musician. God's spirit left Saul, and an evil spirit took hold of him. Saul asked for someone to play music to soothe his soul, and one of Saul's attendants responded that Jesse of Bethlehem had a son who was a skilled musician. So Saul had David brought, and Saul took a liking to him. Whenever Saul was overcome by the evil spirit, David played his lyre, and the evil spirit left Saul. (16:13–23)

David and Goliath. The Philistines again assembled for battle. Their champion was a giant named Goliath of Gath. Goliath proposed that the battle be decided by single combat and challenged any champion of Israel to fight him. In all of Israel, only David volunteered to fight the giant. King Saul offered David his armor, but David refused it. Instead, David went to battle with just his sling and five smooth stones. Goliath mocked the puny warrior that Israel had sent against him. But David slung a stone that struck Goliath in the forehead. Goliath fell to the ground, and David hacked off Goliath's head with the giant's own sword. (Chapter 17)

David's popularity. David and Saul's son Jonathan became close friends. Saul put David in command of his soldiers; but soon, Saul became jealous of David's popularity after killing Goliath. One day, while David was playing music for Saul, in a fit of insanity Saul hurled a spear at David and tried to kill him. (18:1–17)

David's marriage. Saul offered his older daughter Merab to David in marriage. David declined, saying he was unworthy, and Merab married someone else. Saul's younger daughter Michal fell in love with David, and Saul offered her to David in marriage. However, Saul stipulated that first David must prove himself worthy by paying a bride-price of a hundred Philistine foreskins. Saul hoped the Philistines would kill David, but David and his men killed two hundred Philistines. David brought their foreskins to Saul, and he married Michal. (18:18–30)

David is forced to flee. Saul wanted Jonathan to kill David, but Jonathan refused, and he talked Saul out of it. David led the army of Israel to a great victory over the Philistines, and Saul became still more jealous of David. He sent men to David's home at night, with instructions to kill David in the morning. But Michal warned David and helped him escape. When Saul confronted Michal regarding her complicity, she answered that David had threatened to kill her if she didn't help him get away. (19:1–17)

Saul's repeated attempts. David hid out in Samuel's house in Ramah. Saul repeatedly sent messengers there to arrest David. The messengers were unsuccessful, and finally Saul went to Samuel's home himself. But he, too, was unsuccessful, and David escaped. (19:18–24)

Jonathan's warning. Some time later, David asked Jonathan to find out whether Saul was still intent on killing him. On the new moon, David was supposed to dine with Saul, but when David didn't come that day or the next day, Saul asked his son Jonathan for David's whereabouts. Saul got mad at Jonathan for trying to protect David, and he declared that Jonathan's kingship would never be secure so long as David lives. When Jonathan asked what David had done that he deserved to die, Saul hurled a spear at Jonathan. On the following morning, Jonathan went to a field for target practice, and he sent a pre-arranged signal to David, who was hiding in the field. (Chapter 20)

David among the Philistines. David went to the priest Ahimelekh in the city of Nov. David said he was on a secret mission for King Saul, and he asked the priest for provisions and a weapon. Ahimelekh provided David with food, but the only weapon in his house was the sword that David had taken from Goliath, and Ahimelekh invited David to take it. David took the food and Goliath's sword, and he fled to the Philistine city of Gath. But there, the king's courtiers spoke to the king about David's military reputation, and David was afraid that the king of Gath may want to do him harm. Therefore, David feigned insanity. (Chapter 21)

Saul and the priests of Nov. Doeg the Edomite informed Saul that he had seen Ahimelekh provide David with food and with Goliath's sword. So Saul summoned Ahimelekh. Ahimelekh said he thought David was Saul's trusted courtier and denied conspiring against Saul. Saul commanded his guards to put Ahimelekh and his entire family to death. When the guards refused, Saul commanded Doeg the Edomite to do so. So Doeg killed Ahimelekh and 85 men—all the priests of the city of Nov—as well as all their wives, children, and livestock. But Abiathar, one of Ahimelekh's sons, escaped, and he fled to David. (Chapter 22)

Jonathan's pact with David. David's army grew, and he used it to defend the local Israelites against the Philistines. Jonathan came to David, and, saying that both he and Saul know David will be king, Jonathan made a pact with David: when David becomes king, he—Jonathan—will be David's viceroy. (Chapter 23)

Saul pursues David. Saul learned that David was in the desert of Ein-Gedi. Saul took 3,000 men and went in pursuit of David. David and his men were in the back of a cave when Saul entered the cave alone, to relieve himself; but David did not allow his men to harm Saul. Instead, David crept up to Saul and cut off the corner of Saul's coat. When Saul was at a distance from the cave, David called out to him and declared that he meant Saul no harm: he could have killed Saul in the cave, but he didn't. Saul was remorseful, and he withdrew. David remained in his stronghold in the desert. (Chapter 24)

The death of Samuel. Samuel died and was buried in his home, in Ramah. (25:1)

Nabal. There was a very wealthy man named Nabal, whose property David's army had previously protected from the Philistines. David now sent messengers to Nabal requesting food and water for his men, but Nabal refused to give them anything. He was rude to the messengers, and spoke disparagingly of David. When the messengers reported Nabal's response, David took 400 men and went to attack Nabal. Meanwhile, Nabal's wife Abigail, who was an intelligent and beautiful woman, heard what had happened, and, without her husband's knowledge, brought David food for his troops and apologized profusely for her husband's uncouth behavior. She gave David her blessing, and David thanked her for preventing him from committing an evil act. Ten days later, God struck Nabal dead, and David proposed marriage to Abigail. She accepted, and he married her. David also married Ahinoam of Jezreel. Meanwhile, Saul gave David's wife Michal to another man. (Chapter 25)

David enters Saul's camp. Saul resumed his pursuit of David. David, with one of his men, sneaked into Saul's camp at night. Saul was asleep, with his spear thrust in the ground nearby. Abner, the commander of Saul's army, slept next to him, and the troops were all around him. David's companion offered to kill Saul, but David answered that no one may kill the Lord's anointed; God will eventually take Saul's life. So they took Saul's spear and a jug of water that lay nearby, and they left undetected. When David was far away, on a facing hill, he called to Abner and reprimanded him for not defending his king. And he pointedly declared that he had taken Saul's spear and water jug, and he could have killed Saul. Saul admitted he was wrong to pursue David. Saul withdrew, and he gave David his blessing. (Chapter 26)

David joins the Philistines. David feared that Saul would resume pursuing him. Therefore David, with 600 men, sought the protection of the Philistine Akhish, king of Gath. David pretended to fight for the Philistines. Akhish came to trust David, and he gave him the fortress of Ziklag. David wiped out several towns of Israel's enemies, leaving none alive to escape and tell Akhish. (Chapter 27)

Saul consults a necromancer. The Philistines assembled a great army to fight against Israel. Saul was much afraid, and he consulted God through the high priest and through prophets, but God did not answer him. In desperation, Saul went in disguise to the sorceress of En-Dor, a necromancer, and asked her to raise the spirit of Samuel from the dead. She did so, and Samuel said to Saul, "Tomorrow, your sons and you will be with me." (Chapter 28)

The Philistines prepare for battle. The Philistines mustered their army, and David and his men were among them. Akhish continued to trust David's loyalty, but the lords of the Philistines didn't trust him, and they persuaded Akhish to send David and his men away. (Chapter 29)

The Amalekites attack the fortress of Ziklag. When David and his men returned to Ziklag, they discovered that in their absence the Amalekites had attacked Ziklag and burnt it to the ground. Also, the Amalekites had taken all the women and children captive, including two of David's wives, Ahinoam and Abigail. David and his men pursued the Amalekites and recovered all their wives and children. (Chapter 30)

Saul's final battle. The Philistines attacked Israel at Mount Gilboa. Three of Saul's sons, including Jonathan, were killed in the battle, and Saul, mortally wounded, fell on his sword. When the Philistines found Saul's body, they cut off his head and impaled the corpse on the wall of Beth-Shan. But during the night, Israelite soldiers recovered his body and buried it. (Chapter 31)

THE SECOND BOOK OF SAMUEL

Note: In some places, additional details from the book of Chronicles *are inserted in italics.*

David learns of Saul's death. An Amalekite man appeared in David's camp at Ziklag and reported the death of Saul and his sons. He said that as Saul was dying during his final battle, he had asked this Amalekite man to finish him off, and the Amalekite had done so. On hearing the news, David mourned Saul's death and had one of his men execute the Amalekite for raising his hand against Saul, who was God's anointed. David composed a poem lamenting the deaths of Saul and Jonathan. (2 Samuel, Chapter 1)

Ish-Bosheth. After consulting the Lord, David went to Hebron in the territory of Judah, and there he was anointed king. But Abner, Saul's army commander, took Saul's youngest son, Ish-Bosheth, and declared him king. Most of Israel followed Ish-Bosheth, and only the tribe of Judah recognized David as king. David settled in Hebron and ruled over Judah for seven years and six months. (2:1–11)

Civil war. Abner led his army to attack Judah, and the war between the House of Saul and the House of David lasted for many months; but David's forces, under the command of his nephew Joab, continued to gain strength. (2:12 – 3:5)

Abner breaks with the House of Saul. Abner continued to support the House of Saul until one day Ish-Bosheth gravely insulted Abner. Abner sent a message to David informing him that he wanted to switch allegiance. David answered that he would accept Abner only on condition that Abner bring with him Saul's daughter Michal, who was David's rightful wife. Abner brought Michal, and he went with twenty men to David in Hebron. David welcomed Abner and made a feast for him, but then he sent Abner away. (3:6–21)

The civil war concludes. When Joab returned from a raid against Ish-Bosheth's army and learned that David had sent Abner away unharmed, he was alarmed, because he distrusted Abner. But Joab also sought revenge against Abner, because Abner had killed Joab's brother in battle. Without David's knowledge, Joab arranged a meeting with Abner; and while talking to Abner, Joab stabbed Abner to death. When David was informed, he cursed Joab. Abner was buried in Hebron, and David declared that on that day a prince and a great man had fallen. (3:22–39)

The fate of Ish-Bosheth. Two of Ish-Bosheth's company commanders assassinated Ish-Bosheth, and they brought his severed head to David. They had expected to win David's praise; but instead, David had them executed for murder. Ish-Bosheth had reigned for two years. (Chapter 4)

King David solidifies his reign. After the death of Ish-Bosheth, all of Israel swore allegiance to David, and he was anointed again in Hebron, as king over all of Israel. King David and his men penetrated the supposedly invincible Jebusite city of Jerusalem and conquered it. And Hiram king of Tyre sent cedar logs, carpenters, and stonemasons to build a palace for King David. After seven years and six months in Hebron, David moved his capital to Jerusalem, where he would reign for 33 more years. David took several more wives and concubines, and he had many sons and daughters. *When the Philistines heard that David had been anointed king over all of Israel, they mobilized against him. David defeated the Philistines in two battles, and all the surrounding nations began to fear David.* (Chapter 5, *and 1 Chronicles 14:8–17*)

David brings the Ark of God to Jerusalem. David ordered the Ark to be loaded on a cart and brought to Jerusalem from the house of Abinadab in the town of Kiriath-Yearim, where it had been for twenty years. But on the way, Abinadab's son Uzza touched the Ark and died. David therefore diverted the Ark to the house of Obed-Edom, and the Lord blessed Obed-Edom's house because of the Ark. After three months, David had the Ark brought to Jerusalem with great fanfare, and David was leaping and dancing in front of the procession that brought the Ark into the city. David's wife Michal saw David from her window, and she thought his behavior repulsive and beneath the dignity of a king. She reprimanded him harshly and with sarcasm. David responded that it was his honor to dance before the Lord, Who had chosen him to rule instead of Michal's father. Michal had no child until the day of her death. (Chapter 6)

David wants to build a Temple. David felt bad that he was living in a palace, while the Ark was residing in a tent. David asked the prophet Nathan whether he should build a Temple, and Nathan agreed. But that night, the Lord told Nathan to tell David that he is not the one to build the Temple, because he is a man of war. However, God said, David's son *will be a man of peace, and he* will build the Temple. And God promised that the kingship will remain in David's family forever. David accepted God's decision; *but David set aside large quantities of gold, silver, and building materials* *in preparation for his son to use in building the Temple.* (Chapter 7, and 1 Chronicles Chapter 22)

King David's military prowess. David defeated the Philistines, the Moabites, the Arameans, the Edomites, and other neighboring kingdoms, and they became his vassals. And David stationed troops in Damascus. (Chapter 8)

Mephibosheth, son of Jonathan. David inquired whether anyone remained from the House of Saul, and he was informed that Jonathan's son Mephibosheth, who was a cripple, was still alive. David had Mephibosheth brought before him, and he assured Mephibosheth that he would be treated well on account of his father Jonathan. David granted Mephibosheth all the land that had belonged to Saul, and people to work the land. And he told Mephibosheth that he would always be welcome to eat at David's table. So Mephibosheth lived in Jerusalem, and he ate frequently at the king's table. (Chapter 9)

War against Ammon. Nahash, King of Ammon, was David's ally. Therefore, when Nahash died, David sent ambassadors to console the new king, Hanun son of Nahash. But Hanun disgraced David's ambassadors. Hanun, realizing that he had provoked a war, asked the Arameans for help. The combined armies of Ammon and Aram attacked Israel, but David's army killed the Aramean commander and defeated the combined enemy forces. (Chapter 10)

David and Bathsheba. David sent his army under the command of Joab to attack Rabbah, the capital of Ammon; but David remained in Jerusalem. From his roof, David saw a beautiful woman bathing. On inquiring, he found out that she was Bathsheba, wife of Uriah the Hittite, who was at that time serving in the army besieging Rabbah. David had Bathsheba brought to him. He lay with her, and she became pregnant. Then David sent a message to Joab, ordering him to send Uriah into battle and assign him to the front lines. Uriah was killed in battle, and, when Bathsheba's period of mourning for Uriah was over, David married her. (Chapter 11)

Nathan rebukes King David. God was angry with David for causing Uriah's death and taking Uriah's wife, and He sent the prophet Nathan to rebuke David. Nathan went to David and told him a story: There was a rich man who had large flocks, and a poor man who had one lamb that he loved. One day, the rich man took the poor man's lamb and slaughtered it to prepare a meal for a guest. David became enraged and said the rich man deserves to die and must be severely punished. To which Nathan responded, "That man is you!" And, Nathan declared, God will punish David. Calamity will befall David's own house, and David's wives will be taken from him to sleep with another. David admitted his sin and was remorseful. Bathsheba gave birth to a son, but the baby soon became ill. David fasted and prayed to God, but the baby died. David and Bathsheba had another son, and they named him Shlomo—Solomon. But God sent Nathan to give the child an additional name: Jedidiah—beloved of the Lord. (12:1–25)

The defeat of Rabbah. David joined the army besieging Rabbah. He captured the city, and the bejeweled golden crown of the Ammonite king was placed on David's head. (12:26–31)

Amnon and Tamar. Amnon, David's firstborn son, fell in love with his beautiful half-sister Tamar. He pretended to be ill and asked that Tamar bring him food. When she came, he tried to seduce her; and when she resisted his advances, he raped her. But afterwards, he despised her, and he sent her away. Two years later, Tamar's full brother Absalom invited Amnon to a party. He got

Amnon drunk and had his men kill Amnon. Then Absalom fled to his maternal grandfather, Talmai king of Geshur, with whom he remained for three years. (Chapter 13)

The return of Absalom. After three years, Joab saw that David missed Absalom greatly. So Joab sent a female petitioner to the king with a fabricated story of her personal family tragedy, and with her help he persuaded David to allow Absalom to return to Jerusalem. Absalom returned, but for another two years David did not consent to see him, and Joab would not speak to him either. Only after Absalom set fire to Joab's field did Joab relent. Joab agreed to speak to David on Absalom's behalf, and he convinced David to make peace with Absalom. (13:39 – 14:33)

Absalom's rebellion. Some time later, Absalom got himself a chariot and horses, and a retinue of fifty men. He asked David for leave to go to Hebron. Absalom took with him David's counselor Ahithophel and 200 men who did not know what Absalom was planning. When he arrived in Hebron, Absalom declared himself king. He won the hearts of his countrymen, and many rallied to his cause. David fled Jerusalem and went to the Mount of Olives. There he encountered a man named Hushai, who was loyal to David and wanted to join David's men. But David instead sent Hushai to join Absalom and serve as a spy. (Chapter 15)

Saul's kinsmen. David encountered Tsiva, the servant of Jonathan's son Mephibosheth. Tsiva came with donkeys laden with food and drink for David and his men. Tsiva also told David that Mephibosheth expected Israel would soon give him the throne of his grandfather Saul, whereupon David declared that henceforth, all that belonged to Mephibosheth would be the property of Tsiva. Soon after, on approaching the town of Bahurim, a member of

Saul's family named Shim'i son of Gera hurled stones, insults, and curses at David, saying that the Lord was paying David back for his crimes against the House of Saul. (16:1–14)

Absalom's arrival in Jerusalem. On Ahithophel's advice, when Absalom arrived in Jerusalem, he took David's concubines to assert his kingship. Ahithophel also advised Absalom to send a force to immediately attack David that very night while David and his men were tired, and Ahithophel himself would kill David. But Hushai advised Absalom to enlist more men from all of Israel, and Absalom himself would lead his army into battle. Instead of taking the better advice of Ahithophel, Absalom adopted Hushai's plan. Hushai secretly sent word to David, and David moved his men across the Jordan River. When Ahithophel learned that Absalom had not taken his advice, he went home and killed himself. And Absalom appointed Amasa—who was a cousin to both Joab and Absalom—as commander of his army. (16:15 – 17:29)

The death of Absalom. Absalom's army fought a battle against David's supporters in the forest of Ephraim. David's troops were outnumbered, but they were well-trained and hardened fighters, and Absalom's army was routed. Absalom fled, riding on a mule. When the mule passed under a tree, Absalom's long hair caught on a branch, and he was suspended in mid-air as the mule kept going. And, despite David's admonition to spare his son, Joab stabbed Absalom three times in the heart and flung his body into a pit. David mourned the death of Absalom, saying he wished he himself had died instead. (18:1 – 19:11)

The return of King David. David crossed the Jordan and headed back to Jerusalem. He appointed his nephew Amasa as commander of his army, replacing Joab. On the way, many people accompanied

David. (19:12–44)

Another rebellion. A man named Sheba from the tribe of Benjamin incited another rebellion, and only the tribe of Judah remained loyal to David. David sent his army commander Amasa to assemble the men of Judah, and he sent Joab and his brother to pursue Sheba. On the way, Joab and his men encountered Amasa. Joab approached Amasa, as if to kiss him, and he thrust his sword into Amasa's belly, killing him. Joab tracked down Sheba, had him killed, and quelled the rebellion. David reinstated Joab as commander of the army. (Chapter 20)

Renewed war against the Philistines. War again broke out between the Philistines and Israel. Among the Philistines were four men from the city of Gath who were descendants of a race of giants, and David's mighty warriors killed all four, *including Goliath's brother*. When the fighting concluded, David composed a poem thanking the Lord for saving him from all his enemies as well as from Saul. (Chapters 21–23, *and 1 Chronicles 20:5*)

A census. King David ordered Joab to take a census. Joab questioned the order, but David persisted, and Joab conducted the census. Joab reported the count as 800,000 men of Israel who were fit to go to war, plus 500,000 men of Judah. After the count was completed, David realized that he had sinned by ordering the census. God brought a pestilence in punishment, *and David saw an angel with a drawn sword poised over Jerusalem*. When the pestilence was about to enter Jerusalem, the prophet Gad advised David to build an altar and sacrifice to the Lord. So David set up the altar, brought the burnt offering and prayed to the Lord. The pestilence ended, *and the angel re-sheathed his sword*. (Chapter 24, *and 1 Chronicles Chapter 21*)

THE FIRST BOOK OF KINGS

Note: In some places, additional details from the book of Chronicles *are inserted in italics.*

Adonijah. When David was old, he could not keep warm. A beautiful young woman named Avishag was brought to him, to keep him warm and attend to him. At that time, David's son Adonijah, who was born next after Absalom and was the son of David's wife Haggith, declared himself to be the future king, and Joab supported Adonijah's claim. Adonijah made a feast, to which he invited all the other princes except his brother Solomon. The prophet Nathan knew that David had sworn to Bathsheba that her son Solomon would succeed him as king. And so, on Nathan's advice, Bathsheba went to David and informed him that Adonijah had declared himself king. As Bathsheba was speaking, Nathan entered and confirmed her words. David immediately commanded that Solomon ride on the king's mule down to the spring of Gihon, where the priest Zadok and the prophet Nathan will anoint Solomon as king. *David assembled all the people and announced that God had chosen Solomon his son to succeed him as king and to build a Temple to the Lord. David blessed Solomon and gave him detailed plans for building the Temple, as the Lord had instructed David.* Solomon sat upon the king's throne, a *shofar* was sounded, and the people proclaimed, "Long live King Solomon!" When Adonijah was informed that David had had Solomon anointed king, he feared for his life. But Solomon declared that as long as Adonijah behaves as a loyal subject, he will not be harmed. (1 Kings, Chapter 1, and *1 Chronicles Chapters 28 & 29*)

King David's last wishes. When King David was about to die, he called for Solomon and told him that he must always follow God's ways and observe the Torah's commandments. And David warned his son what he must do to secure his throne. Solomon must be sure to kill Joab, because he had murdered the two army commanders Abner and Amasa; and Solomon must also kill Shim'i son of Gera, who had cursed David when David was fleeing from Saul. David died and was buried in the City of David. (2:1–12)

Solomon secures his throne. Adonijah went to Bathsheba, and, after remarking that the throne was rightfully his but the Lord wanted otherwise, he requested that Bathsheba ask Solomon to allow Adonijah to marry Avishag, who had been King David's attendant. Solomon realized that Adonijah still wanted the throne, and he had Benaiah—one of David's mightiest warriors—kill Adonijah. Solomon also sent Benaiah to kill Joab; and Solomon appointed Benaiah as army commander. Finally, Solomon ordered Shim'i that he must never leave Jerusalem, on pain of death; and Shim'i agreed. But three years later, Shim'i left Jerusalem, and Solomon had him killed. Thus, King Solomon secured his throne. (2:13–46)

Pharaoh's daughter. Solomon made an alliance with Egypt. He married Pharaoh's daughter and brought her to live in Jerusalem. (3:1)

Solomon's dream. King Solomon had a dream in which God told him to request anything he desired. Solomon requested a discerning heart, to distinguish good from evil and to judge wisely. God praised Solomon's choice and said that because Solomon had chosen so well, God would also grant him great wealth and great repute. (3:2–15)

King Solomon's judgement. Two prostitutes came before the king. The first one said she had given birth to a son, and three days later the other woman also gave birth to a son. But the other woman's baby died, and she switched the babies. Each woman claimed the living baby to be her own. Solomon had a sword brought. He proposed to cut the living baby in two, and give half to each woman. The woman who was the true mother immediately pleaded with the king to let the baby live and be given to the other woman, whereupon Solomon awarded the baby to her, saying, "She is the mother." (3:16–28)

Solomon's kingdom. King Solomon ruled over all the lands west of the Euphrates River, to the territory of the Philistines and the border of Egypt, from Dan in the north to Beer-Sheba in the south. And all of Israel and Judea lived in peace and security throughout Solomon's reign. King Hiram of Tyre, who had been an ally of King David, sent cedar and cypress wood for Solomon to build a temple to the Lord, and Solomon paid Hiram in food. (4:1 – 5:25)

Solomon's Temple. The Lord gave Solomon wisdom as He had promised. Solomon made a treaty with Hiram, and Hiram's workers helped the people of Israel in building the Temple. In the innermost part of the building was the Holy of Holies, in which would be placed the Ark of the Covenant of the Lord, and a pair of Cherubim made of olive-wood overlaid with gold, each with a wingspan of ten cubits. The doors to the inner sanctum were also of olive-wood overlaid with pure gold. The entire structure was completed in the eleventh year of Solomon's reign. (5:26 – 7:1)

Inauguration of the Temple. When the Temple was completed, Solomon called a convocation of all the elders of Israel, the tribal chiefs, and the clan chieftains; and he had the Ark of the Covenant brought from Zion—the City of David—to the Temple, to the Holy of Holies. The Ark contained only the tablets of the Decalogue that Moses had placed there when he descended from Mount Horeb. When the Ark was placed in the Holy of Holies, the cloud of the Lord's Presence covered the House of the Lord, and the priests had to leave the building. Solomon blessed the people, and he went to the altar. He knelt and prayed to God, and he thanked God for enabling him to build a Temple for the Lord's worship. And when he finished praying, he rose from his knees. *Then, a fire descended from heaven and consumed the offerings on the altar, and the Lord's presence filled the building. Thereupon, the people bowed and praised the Lord,* and all of Israel rejoiced with Solomon for fourteen days. (7:2 – 8:66, *and 2 Chronicles 7:1–3*)

Pharaoh's daughter's dowry. Pharaoh conquered the Canaanite city of Gezer and gave it to his daughter as dowry. And Solomon built a palace for Pharaoh's daughter in Gezer. (9:1–25)

King Solomon's defenses, and his fleet. Solomon *built fortified cities and military garrisons in the desert and in the part of Lebanon that he ruled. He* built a fleet of ships in the land of Edom on the shore of the Red Sea, and Hiram sent experienced sailors to serve alongside Solomon's men. They sailed to the land of Ophir, where they obtained a large amount of gold for King Solomon. (9:26–28, *and 2 Chronicles 8:1–6*)

The queen of Sheba. The queen of Sheba heard of Solomon's fame. She came with a large retinue, and with great quantities of gold and precious stones. She was very impressed with Solomon's wisdom and his administration of justice. She gave Solomon large amounts of gold, spices, and precious stones; and he gave her whatever she wanted. Then she and her retinue left and returned home. (10:1–13)

The king's throne, and his wealth. King Solomon's throne was very ornate, made of ivory overlaid with gold, with six steps leading up to the throne. A pair of lions stood at the sides of the throne, and a lion stood on either side of each of the six steps. His fleet brought much gold, silver, monkeys, and peacocks from Tarshish. And he had 1,4000 chariots and 12,000 horses. (10:14–29)

King Solomon sins. King Solomon loved many foreign women, and he married many foreign princesses, who led him astray. When he became old, he was drawn to the gods of other nations. Consequently, God sent the prophet Ahijah of Shiloh to Jeroboam, one of Solomon's labor foremen, to appoint Jeroboam king over the ten northern tribes of Israel. Solomon tried to kill Jeroboam, but Jeroboam fled to Egypt, where he remained until Solomon's death. (Chapter 11)

The kingdom is divided. When Solomon died, his son Rehoboam became king. The people petitioned him to ease the tax burden that Solomon had imposed on them. The elders who had served under Solomon advised Rehoboam to accede to the people's demand. But Rehoboam instead listened to the advice of the youths who had grown up with him, and he answered that he would increase the tax: "My father chastised you with whips, but I will chastise you with scorpions." Thereupon, the people of Israel rejected the House of David; and Jeroboam, who had returned from exile in Egypt, became their king. But the tribe of Judah remained faithful to Rehoboam. Rehoboam mustered 180,000 troops from the tribes of Judah and Benjamin—which were now the Kingdom of Judea—to war against the ten northern tribes, the Kingdom of Israel. But Shemaiah, a man of God, declared that the Lord forbade waging war against their brothers. The troops dispersed and returned to their homes. (12:1–24)

The two golden calves. Jeroboam was afraid that his subjects would bring offerings to the Temple in Jerusalem and would be drawn to return to the House of David. Therefore, Jeroboam had two golden calves made—one to be placed in Dan, and the other in Bethel—and the people were to worship there instead of in Jerusalem. He declared: "These are your gods, Israel, who brought you up from the land of Egypt." And he proclaimed a new festival on the fifteenth day of the eighth month. (12:25–33)

The altar at Bethel. As Jeroboam was about to make an offering on the altar at Bethel, a man of God appeared from Judea and prophesied that a son will be born to the House of David, named Josiah; and he will destroy the idolatrous shrines and execute its priests. And the man of God gave a sign: the altar will break apart. Jeroboam stretched out his arm and said, "Seize him!" But his arm became rigid, and he couldn't draw it back. At Jeroboam's request, the man of God prayed to the Lord, and Jeroboam's arm returned to normal. Immediately, the altar broke apart, and its ashes spilled upon the ground. But even after that incident, Jeroboam did not relent, and he continued to appoint non-Levite priests for his pagan cult. (Chapter 13)

The death of Jeroboam's son. Jeroboam's son became ill, and Jeroboam sent his wife in disguise to the prophet Ahijah to ask what will happen to his son. Ahijah was now blind, but God told him that Jeroboam's wife was coming, and Ahijah told her God's message: Jeroboam has violated his charge, has violated the Lord's commands, and has led his people astray. Therefore, God will bring disaster upon his house. His sick son will die. The kingship will be torn away from the house of Jeroboam, and the people of Israel will eventually be exiled because of their sins. Just as Jeroboam's wife returned home, their son died. Jeroboam reigned for 22 years, and his son Nadab succeeded him. (14:1–20)

Rehoboam, king of Judea. Rehoboam, son of Solomon, reigned in Jerusalem for 17 years. In his fifth year, King Shishak of Egypt attacked Jerusalem. He took away the treasures of the House of the Lord and of the palace. There was war between Rehoboam and Jeroboam throughout Rehoboam's reign. (14:21–31)

Rehoboam's sons. Rehoboam's son Abijam (*"Abijah" in 2 Chronicles, Chapter 13*) was sinful. He reigned for three years, and his brother Asa succeeded him as King of Judea. Asa was a righteous king, and he reigned for 41 years. He removed the idols and altars to alien gods, *and he made a pact with the people of Judea to worship the Lord and obey His commandments.* And he deposed his mother from her position as queen mother, because she had made an idol of Asherah. (15:1–15, and *2 Chronicles Chapter 15*)

Jeroboam's legacy. Meanwhile, in the Kingdom of Israel, Jeroboam's son Nadab became king. But two years later, a man named Baasha killed Nadab, massacred all of Nadab's family, and became king of Israel. King Baasha went on to attack the kingdom of Judea, and the Judean king Asa sent a payment of silver and gold to his ally King Ben-Hadad of Aram, requesting his help. Ben-Hadad sent his army against the kingdom of Israel, and Baasha withdrew. Baasha reigned for 24 years, and he followed in Jeroboam's evil ways. (15:16–34)

Zimri and Omri. After the death of Baasha, his son Elah became king of Israel. After a reign of two years, Zimri, one of his chariot commanders, assassinated him and killed his entire family and all his friends. But Zimri reigned for only seven days. When the troops heard of Zimri's insurrection, they crowned Omri, the army commander, as King of Israel. Zimri fled to the royal palace and set it on fire, with himself inside. Omri reigned for twelve years, and he built the city of Samaria (Shomron). His evil exceeded that of all the previous kings of Israel, and he died in the 38th year of Asa king of Judea. Omri's son Ahab, who succeeded him as King of Israel, was even more evil than his father. He married Jezebel, the daughter of the king of the Phoenician city of Sidon. He worshipped the Phoenician god Baal, and he built an altar and a temple to Baal in Samaria. (Chapter 16)

Elijah the prophet. The Lord sent the prophet Elijah to Ahab, saying there will be no more rain in Samaria until God decrees it. Elijah was forced to flee, first to a wadi in the desert and later to Sidon, where he stayed at the home of a certain widow. Some time later, the widow's son got sick, and his breathing ceased. The woman asked Elijah what harm she had done him that he had brought about her son's death. But Elijah took the boy, prayed to God, and miraculously revived the boy. (Chapter 17)

Elijah's challenge. Queen Jezebel had the prophets of God killed. But Obadiahu, the palace chamberlain, hid a hundred of the prophets in caves, and he sustained them with food and water. In the third year of drought, the Lord sent Elijah to Ahab to tell him that there will be rain. Elijah admonished the king for his worship of Baal, and he challenged King Ahab to summon 450 prophets of Baal to a contest against Elijah at Mount Carmel, to prove which is the true God. The prophets of Baal placed their offering on an altar, and Elijah placed his offering on another altar. Elijah told the prophets of Baal to pray to Baal to send a fire to consume the sacrifice. But Baal did not answer. Elijah then poured water over his offering and proceeded to pray to the Lord. A fire descended from heaven and consumed both the sacrifice and the altar. Elijah commanded the people to seize the prophets of Baal, and Elijah killed them all. (Chapter 18)

Elijah flees the wrath of Jezebel. Queen Jezebel threatened to kill Elijah for his killing of the prophets of Baal. Elijah fled into the desert; and, after a forty-day trek, he arrived at Mount Horeb, the Mountain of God. The Lord asked Elijah why he had come, to which Elijah replied that Israel had forsaken the Lord and killed His prophets, and only Elijah remained to fight for the Lord. In answer, God told Elijah to do three things: to go to Damascus and anoint a new king of Aram; to anoint a new king of the Kingdom of Israel; and to appoint Elisha son of Shaphat to succeed Elijah as prophet. (Elijah did appoint Elisha as his successor, but God's other two commands were left for Elisha to carry out later.) (19:1–18)

Elisha. Elijah returned from the desert and found Elisha son of Shaphat plowing his field. Elijah threw his cloak upon Elisha. Elisha bade farewell to his parents and followed Elijah. (19:19–21)

War with Aram. Ben-Hadad, king of Aram, besieged Samaria and threatened to lay waste to the city. In the ensuing battle, Ahab vanquished the Aramean army. But Aram re-armed, and at the end of the year they attacked Israel again. Again the Arameans were routed, and Ben-Hadad surrendered. King Ahab let him live and made a treaty with him. (Chapter 20)

The vineyard of Navoth. A man named Navoth owned a vineyard adjoining King Ahab's palace. Ahab offered to buy the vineyard, but Navoth refused to sell his ancestral property. So Queen Jezebel had two men testify falsely against Navoth. Navoth was convicted of a capital offense and executed, and Ahab seized his property. At the Lord's command, Elijah went to Ahab and rebuked him for the murder of Navoth and the seizure of his vineyard. Because of his sins, Elijah declared, God will put Ahab to death and will put an end to his line. Ahab tore his garments. He fasted, and he repented of his crime. God therefore told Elijah that He would allow Ahab's line to continue for one more generation. (Chapter 21)

Ahab's death. After three years of peace, Ahab decided to attack Aram, and he asked the Judean king, Jehoshaphat son of Asa, to join him in battle. Despite a prophecy spoken before both kings, that Israel would be scattered among the mountains like sheep without a shepherd, Jehoshaphat went into battle together with Ahab. Ahab was killed by a random Aramean arrow, and his son Ahaziah succeeded him as King of Israel. Ahaziah reigned for two years, and he continued in his father's evil ways. Meanwhile, the Judean king Jehoshaphat returned to Jerusalem. He reigned for 25 years, and he followed the path of righteousness. (Chapter 22)

THE SECOND BOOK OF KINGS

Note: In some places, additional details from the book of Chronicles *are inserted in italics.*

Ahaziah, son of Ahab. King Ahaziah fell through the lattice of his balcony and was severely injured. So he sent messengers to the Philistine city of Ekron to inquire of the idol Baal-Zevuv whether he will survive. On God's command, Elijah intercepted Ahaziah's messengers, and Elijah sent them back to the king, saying, "Is there no God in Israel, that you must go to inquire of Baal-Zevuv the god of Ekron?" Hence, Elijah said, Ahaziah will not rise from his bed, but he will die. And so it was. Ahaziah had no son, and his brother Jehoram succeeded him as King of Israel. (2 Kings, Chapter 1)

Elijah ascends to heaven. Elijah, along with fifty disciples, went with Elisha to the Jordan River. Elijah rolled up his mantle and struck the river. The waters parted, and Elijah crossed with Elisha on the dry riverbed, leaving the disciples behind. Then, as Elijah and Elisha went onward, a fiery chariot drawn by fiery horses appeared, and it separated the two of them. Elijah mounted the chariot and ascended to heaven. Elisha picked up Elijah's mantle that had fallen from him, and Elisha succeeded Elijah as the great prophet of Israel. (Chapter 2)

War against Moab. Jehoram became king of Israel in the eighteenth year of the Judean king Jehoshaphat. The king of Moab used to pay an annual tribute to Israel; but when Ahab died, King Mesha of Moab rebelled and refused to pay the tribute. So Jehoram marched against Moab, together with Jehoshaphat king of Judea, and with the king of Edom. The Moabites suffered a major defeat, and Mesha the Moabite king sacrificed his firstborn son as a burnt offering to his god before the army of Israel withdrew. (Chapter 3)

Elisha performs a miracle. A certain rich, childless woman built an annex to her house for Elisha to use whenever he would pass through her town. Elisha blessed her and said that on the following year she and her husband would have a son, and so she did. After several years, when the boy was in the field with his father, the boy complained of a headache and died later that day. The woman saddled her donkey and went to fetch Elisha. Elisha brought the child back to life. (Chapter 4)

The Aramean commander. Naaman, the commander of the army of Aram, was a leper. A certain captive Israelite girl told Naaman's wife that there was a prophet in Samaria who might cure him. So Naaman sent messengers to the king of Israel, with a large payment of silver and gold, requesting that he be cured. The king of Israel thought Naaman's request was a pretext to start a war, but Elisha agreed to cure Naaman. Elisha told him that when he bathes in the Jordan River seven times, he will be cured, and so it was. Naaman then declared that there is no god but the God of Israel, and he offered to pay Elisha, but Elisha refused. However, after Naaman left, Elisha's servant Gehazi chased after Naaman and said his master wanted payment after all. Gehazi named his price, and Naaman paid him double what he had requested. But when Gehazi returned, Elisha knew what his servant had been up to. He cursed Gehazi, that Naaman's leprosy would fall upon him. And Gehazi became a leper. (Chapter 5)

The siege of Samaria. Some time later, Ben-Hadad king of Aram besieged Samaria, and consequently there was famine in Samaria, and high inflation. Elisha predicted that on the following day flour would again sell for a pittance. That evening, God caused the Arameans to hear the sound of a large army advancing toward them with chariots and horses. The Aramean army fled in disarray; and by the next day, the inflation abated as Elisha had prophesied. (Chapters 6 & 7)

Hazael becomes king of Aram. Elisha went to Damascus, the capital of Aram. King Ben-Hadad was ill, and he sent a royal servant named Hazael to Elisha to ask whether he would recover. Elisha told Hazael that he had foreseen Ben-Hadad's death, but Hazael should tell the king that he will recover. Elisha began to cry, and he told Hazael that he had also foreseen Hazael would be king and would do great harm to Israel. Hazael returned to the king and told him he would recover. On the following day, Hazael suffocated Ben-Hadad, and Hazael became king of Aram. (8:1–15)

The two Jehorams. In the fifth year of Jehoram king of Israel, another Jehoram—Jehoram son of Jehoshaphat—became king of Judea; *and soon after becoming king, the Judean King Jehoram killed all of his brothers.* Jehoram of Judea married Atalia, daughter of Ahab, and he followed in Ahab's evil ways. *A letter from Elijah the prophet arrived, detailing how God will punish the Judean Jehoram for his evil. And, true to Elijah's warning, the Philistines and the Arabians attacked Judea and carried off Jehoram's wives and most of his sons. As Elijah had prophesied, Jehoram of Judea fell ill with a severe affliction of his bowels, from which he died after two years*; and his son Ahaziah succeeded him. Ahaziah was evil as well, and he reigned in Jerusalem for only one year. He joined King Jehoram of Israel in a battle against the Aramean king Hazael. Jehoram of Israel was wounded in the battle, and King Ahaziah of Judea went to visit him. *(8:16–29, and 2 Chronicles 21:4 & 21:12-19)*

Jehu. During the war against Aram, Elisha sent one of his disciples to anoint an army commander named Jehu as King of Israel. Jehu immediately left camp and went to Jezreel, where King Jehoram was recovering from his wounds. Jehu shot an arrow and killed Jehoram; and the Judean king Ahaziah, who was still there visiting, tried to flee. Jehu pursued him, and one of Jehu's men wounded Ahaziah. Ahaziah died soon after and was buried in Jerusalem. Jehu returned to Jezreel where he had his men kill Queen Jezebel, wife of Ahab. And the dogs ate Jezebel's flesh, as Elijah had prophesied. *(Chapter 9)*

Jehu and the prophets of Baal. Ahab had seventy sons, and Jehu had all of them killed. Then he declared that Ahab had worshipped Baal a little, but he—Jehu—would worship Baal a lot. He called for a great feast of Baal, and he summoned the prophets of Baal from all of Israel, on pain of death, to assemble in the temple of Baal. He had eighty soldiers stationed around the temple, and as soon as the sacrifice to Baal was brought, Jehu had his soldiers enter the temple and kill them all. And he had the temple of Baal torn down. Thus Jehu eliminated the worship of Baal in the Kingdom of Israel. But he continued to worship the two golden calves that Jeroboam had erected in Bethel and in Dan. Jehu reigned for 22 years in Samaria, and his son Jehoahaz succeeded him. *(Chapter 10)*

King Joash of Judea. When Queen Atalia saw that her son Ahaziah was dead, she killed all his potential successors, and she usurped the throne. But King Ahaziah's sister Jehosheva managed to save Ahaziah's son Joash, and she hid him in the Temple for six years. When Joash was seven years old, Jehoiada the High Priest orchestrated a rebellion. He had the temple of Baal and all its idols demolished. He had Joash anointed king of Judea, and he had the King's Guard put Atalia to death. Joash reigned in Jerusalem for 40 years, and while Jehoiada lived he followed the righteous ways that Jehoiada had taught him. *But after Jehoiada's death, Joash allowed idolatry to proliferate in Judea. And when Jehoiada's son prophesied against the heathen practices, Joash had him assassinated. During the reign of Joash of Judea,* Hazael king of Aram attacked the city of Gath and advanced against Jerusalem. So Joash paid Hazael a large amount of gold, and Hazael withdrew. Shortly after, two of Joash's courtiers assassinated him, and his son Amaziah succeeded him as King of Judea. (Chapters 11 &12, *and 2 Chronicles 24:17–22*)

Another King Joash. In the 23rd year of King Joash of Judea, Jehoahaz son of Jehu became king of Israel in Samaria. He continued in the sins of the former kings of Israel, and the Lord repeatedly delivered Israel into the hands of the Aramean king Hazael. But after Hazael died, Jehoahaz's son and successor, King Joash of Israel, managed to recapture several cities from Hazael's son. (Chapter 13)

Amaziah's reign. In the second year of King Joash of Israel, Amaziah became king of Judea at the age of 25, and he reigned for 29 years in Jerusalem. When he felt secure in his reign, he put to death the men who had conspired against his father, but, in accordance with the Torah, he did not put their children to death. Amaziah defeated Edom in battle. He then challenged Joash king of Israel to a war. In the ensuing battle, the Judean army was routed, and Amaziah was captured. Joash of Israel marched on Jerusalem and carried off gold, silver, and hostages. Joash returned to Samaria but died soon after, and his son Jeroboam II succeeded him as King of Israel. Amaziah returned to Jerusalem and reigned for fifteen more years as King of Judea. King Amaziah was assassinated, and his son Azariah succeeded him. (14:1–22)

Jeroboam II. Jeroboam II, son of Joash, became king of Israel in the fifteenth year of the Judean king Amaziah. Jeroboam II reigned in Samaria for 41 years, and he followed in the evil ways of the first Jeroboam. He was a great conqueror, and, pursuant to God's promise spoken through the prophet Jonah, he extended the borders of Israel northwards to Hamath, and he also annexed Damascus. Jeroboam II was succeeded by his son Zechariah. (14:23–29)

Azariah (Uzziahu), king of Judea. In the 27th year of Jeroboam II of Israel, Azariah son of Amaziah became king of Judea. Azariah (later called Uzziahu) was sixteen years old when he became king. He was a righteous king, and he reigned for 52 years in Jerusalem. He restored Elath to Judean rule, and *he won battles against Philistines and Arabians. He had a large army, and he built towers and fortifications in Jerusalem and in the desert. But as his power increased, he became arrogant. He entered the Temple and attempted to offer incense on the altar—a task that was the sole prerogative of the priests. For this grave transgression, God punished him*: he became a leper, and his son Jotham administered the kingdom until his death. (14:21–22 & 15:1–7, *and 2 Chronicles 14:3–23*)

Three kings of Israel. Zechariah son of Jeroboam II of Israel was evil, but after six months a man named Shallum assassinated him and became king of Israel. And one month later, Menahem son of Gadi marched on Samaria and killed Shallum. In the 39th year of Uzziahu king of Judea, Menahem became king of Israel, following in the evil ways of his predecessors. In his time, King Pul (Tiglath-Pileser) of Assyria invaded. Menahem paid him a large tribute, and the Assyrian army withdrew. Menahem ruled in Samaria for ten years, and his son Pekahiah succeeded him. (15:8–22)

Pekahiah and Pekah. In the 50th year of the Judean king Azariah, Pekahiah became king of Israel, and he followed in the sinful ways of Jeroboam I. After a reign of two years, Pekah son of Remaliahu assassinated him and declared himself king. Pekah became king of Israel in the 52nd year of the Judean king Azariah, and he continued in the evil ways of his predecessors. In his time, King Tiglath-Pileser of Assyria captured several cities in Gilead and Galilee, and he deported their inhabitants to Assyria. After a reign of twenty years, Pekah was killed by Hoshea son of Elah, who then became king of Israel. (15:23–31)

Jotham, king of Judea. After the death of Uzziahu (Azariah), his son Jotham became king of Judea in Jerusalem; and, like his father, he was a righteous king. In his time, Aram and Israel began to harass Judea. After a reign of sixteen years, Jotham died, and his son Ahaz succeeded him as king of Judea. (15:32–38)

Ahaz. In the seventeenth year of Pekah king of Israel, Ahaz son of Jotham became king of Judea at the age of twenty, and he reigned in Jerusalem for sixteen years. He worshipped pagan deities, and he passed his son through fire in a pagan ritual. In his time, King Retzin of Aram and King Pekah of Israel advanced against

Jerusalem and laid siege to the city. Also, Aram captured the city of Elath, and Edomites settled there. Over the objection of the prophet Isaiah (as stated in Isaiah, Chapter 7), Ahaz sent silver and gold to King Tiglath-Pileser of Assyria and requested his help. So Tiglath-Pileser invaded Aram, attacked its capital Damascus, exiled its inhabitants, and killed King Retzin. Ahaz went to Damascus to meet Tiglath-Pileser, and when he saw the altar there, he had a replica of that altar built in Jerusalem to replace the great altar in the Temple. Ahaz died, and his son Hezekiah succeeded him as king of Judea. (Chapter 16)

The last king of Israel. In the twelfth year of King Ahaz of Judea, Hoshea son of Elah became king of Israel in Samaria. He was sinful, although not as evil as his predecessors. King Shalmaneser of Assyria advanced against Samaria, and Hoshea became his vassal. But the Assyrian king later discovered that Hoshea was conspiring with the king of Egypt to rebel against Assyria. Shalmaneser again attacked Israel and besieged Samaria for three years. And God delivered Israel into the hands of Assyria. Despite many warnings of the prophets, the people of Israel had continued to do wicked acts, to sacrifice to Baal and other idols, to practice sorcery, and to pass their sons and daughters through fire as offerings to a pagan deity. Therefore, in the ninth year of King Hoshea, the Assyrians captured Samaria and exiled the people of Israel to Assyria and lands beyond. And of the original tribes of Israel, only the Kingdom of Judea remained. (17:1–23)

Repopulation of Samaria. The king of Assyria brought people from Babylonia, Cutha, Hamath, and other places, and he resettled them in the cities of Samaria. But the Lord sent lions, and the lions killed some of them. They believed that the God of their new land was angry, because they were not living according to His laws. So the Assyrian king sent them a priest from the exiled Israelites, to teach them how to worship the Lord. The new residents of Samaria began to worship the Lord; but in addition, they continued to worship their former deities, bringing animal sacrifices—and sometimes human sacrifices—to those deities. (17:24–41)

King Hezekiah. In the third year of Hoshea king of Israel, Hezekiah son of Ahaz became king of Judea, at the age of 25. He was a righteous king who turned his nation to the worship of the Lord, and he reigned in Jerusalem for 29 years. He abolished pagan worship in his domain, and, because many Israelites worshipped the copper serpent that Moses had made, he also destroyed the copper serpent. He was committed to serving the Lord and observing His commandments, and the Lord was always with him. Hezekiah strengthened his kingdom, and he conquered the Philistines. In the sixth year of his reign, the Assyrian king conquered Samaria and exiled its people; but Assyria did not advance against Judea at that time. (18:1–12)

The siege of Jerusalem. At a later time, Hezekiah rebelled and refused to serve Assyria., and in the fourteenth year of Hezekiah, the Assyrian king Sennacherib attacked all the fortified cities of Judea. Hezekiah sent him a large payment and asked him to withdraw. *Hezekiah, anticipating an attack against Jerusalem, stopped the flow of water from the springs outside the city, to deprive the enemy of drinking water.* The Assyrians continued to advance against Jerusalem and besieged it. They spoke threatening words and taunted Hezekiah, saying that just as the gods of other nations had not prevailed against Assyria, Hezekiah's God will also be powerless against them. Hezekiah feared greatly, but the prophet Isaiah reassured him that the Assyrian army will withdraw, and the Assyrian king will return to Assyria, where he will die by the sword. Hezekiah prayed to the Lord, and Isaiah sent a message to Hezekiah saying that the Lord had heard his prayer and would protect Jerusalem. That night, an angel of the Lord struck down 185,000 Assyrian soldiers, and in the morning the remainder of the Assyrian army withdrew. King Sennacherib returned to Assyria; and subsequently, while he was worshiping in the temple of one of his gods, two of his sons assassinated him. Those two sons fled, and Esarhaddon—another one of Sennacherib's sons—succeeded him as king. (18:7, 18:13 – 19:37, *and 2 Chronicles Chapter 32*)

Hezekiah's illness. King Hezekiah became deathly ill. Isaiah told him he will not recover. But Hezekiah prayed to God, and God sent Isaiah back to tell the king that because of his fervent prayer, he will recover, and God will grant him fifteen more years of life. (20:1–11)

Babylonian emissaries. During Hezekiah's illness, the king of Babylonia sent emissaries to Hezekiah, along with a gift to wish him well. On his recovery, Hezekiah gave the Babylonian emissaries a tour of the palace and showed them everything, including all its treasures. The Lord sent Isaiah to the palace, and Isaiah told Hezekiah that because of Hezekiah's indiscretion, all the treasures in the palace will be carried away to Babylonia. Also, Isaiah said, some of Hezekiah's progeny will be made into eunuchs to serve in the Babylonian palace. But none of those events will come to pass during Hezekiah's lifetime. Hezekiah strengthened Jerusalem and built a new water conduit in the event of a siege. When Hezekiah died, his son Manasseh succeeded him. (20:12–21)

Manasseh son of Hezekiah. Manasseh became king at age twelve, and he reigned for 55 years. He was an evil king, who did not heed the warnings of prophets. He worshipped idols, he placed an idol in the Temple, he practiced sorcery, he passed his son through fire in a pagan ritual, and he spilled the blood of many. *Because of his sins, the Lord caused the Assyrian army to take Manasseh captive and lead him away in chains. While he was held captive, he repented and prayed to the Lord. The Lord accepted his prayer and returned him to his kingdom in Jerusalem.* When Manasseh died, his son Amon succeeded him. (21:1–14, and *2 Chronicles 33:10–20*)

Amon son of Manasseh. Amon continued in his father's evil ways *but did not repent as his father had done*. He was 22 years old when he became king, and he reigned for two years in Jerusalem. He was assassinated, and the people crowned his son Josiah as his successor. (21:15–26, *and 2 Chronicles 33:21–25*)

Josiah. Josiah became king at the age of eight, and he reigned for 31 years in Jerusalem. In the *eighth year of his reign he began to seek the Lord*, and in the eighteenth year of his reign a scroll of the Torah was found in the Temple. When the scroll was read to Josiah, he was moved to repentance. He tore his clothes and sent men to Hulda the prophetess, to inquire how to avert the Lord's punishment of his people for their sins. And Hulda assured the king that because of his sincere repentance, the Lord will not bring disaster upon the kingdom during Josiah's lifetime. Josiah abolished sorcery, he removed all the idols from the kingdom of Judea, and he turned the people's hearts to God. He removed and destroyed the idols of Baal and Asherah that were in the Temple of the Lord, and he destroyed the Topheth, which was a site in the Valley of Hinnom where children were passed through fire as an offering to the god Molekh. He also destroyed the altar and the idolatrous shrine that the first Jeroboam had erected in Bethel. Josiah was a righteous king, and he was scrupulous in keeping the Lord's commandments. Never before or after him was there a king who returned to the Lord as he did, with all his heart and with all his soul. (22:1 – 23:27, *and 2 Chronicles 34:1–3*)

King Josiah's death. Pharaoh Necho, king of Egypt, marched against Assyria, and, along the way, Josiah confronted the Egyptian army. *Necho sent messengers to Josiah saying he had no quarrel with Josiah, and Josiah should withdraw. But Josiah persisted, and* he was killed in battle. His son Jehoahaz succeeded him. (23:28–30, *and 2 Chronicles 35:20–27*)

Jehoahaz. Jehoahaz was 23 years old when he became king. Unlike his father, he was sinful, and he reigned in Jerusalem for three months. Pharaoh Necho imprisoned him and crowned his brother Eliakim as king of Judea. Pharaoh Necho changed Eliakim's name to Jehoiakim. (23:31–35)

Jehoiakim and Jehoiachin. Jehoiakim was 25 years old when he became king. He was a sinful king, and he reigned in Jerusalem for eleven years. In his time, King Nebuchadnezzar of Babylonia conquered Judea, and Jehoiakim became his vassal; but after three years, Jehoiakim rebelled. Jehoiakim died, and his son Jehoiachin succeeded him. Jehoiachin reigned for only three months. During his reign, Nebuchadnezzar attacked Judea and besieged Jerusalem, and Jehoiachin surrendered. Nebuchadnezzar exiled Jehoiachin, Jehoiachin's mother and wives, all the Judean military commanders, and 10,000 prominent citizens of Jerusalem, sending them all to Babylon. And he took all the treasure stored in the royal palace and in the Temple. Nebuchadnezzar then appointed Jehoiachin's uncle Mattaniah to be king of Judea, and he changed Mattaniah's name to Zedekiah. (23:36 – 24:17)

Zedekiah, the last king of Judea. Zedekiah was 21 years old when he became king, and he reigned for eleven years in Jerusalem. But Zedekiah rebelled against Babylonia, and Nebuchadnezzar sent his army to attack Jerusalem. He sacked Jerusalem, burned the Temple to the ground, and captured Zedekiah. He killed Zedekiah's children before his eyes. Then he blinded Zedekiah and brought him in chains to Babylonia. And the people of Judea were carried off to exile in Babylonia. (24:18 – 25:26)

King Jehoiachin's latter days. In the 37th year of exile of Judean king Jehoiachin, Evill-Merodach succeeded Nebuchadnezzar as king of Babylonia. In the first year of his reign, the new Babylonian king released Jehoiachin from prison and elevated him to a high position. (25:27–30)

King Cyrus of Persia. (Cyrus conquered Babylonia.) *In the first year of Cyrus's rule (over Babylonia), he issued a proclamation saying that the Lord God has ordered him to rebuild the Temple in Jerusalem, and anyone of God's nation who wants to return to Judea may do so. (2 Chronicles 36:22–23)*

ISAIAH

A vision of destruction. Isaiah son of Amotz prophesied during the reigns of Uzziahu, Jotham, Ahaz, and Hezekiah, kings of Judea. Isaiah calls upon heaven and earth as witnesses to his prophecy. God's nation has sinned grievously, and punishment is forthcoming. In his vision, Isaiah sees desolation, and cities burnt by fire. Jerusalem stands alone, the remnant of the tribes of Israel. But if the people of Judea are to avoid destruction, they must repent in earnest. They must no longer pervert justice, they must put a stop to bloodshed, and they must return to follow the way of the Lord. Then, Jerusalem will return to its former greatness and will be known as the city of righteousness. (Isaiah, Chapter 1)

Revival. Isaiah prophesies that in the latter days all nations will flock to Zion (*i.e.* Jerusalem), to learn God's ways and to follow His teachings. They will beat their swords into ploughshares, and there will be no more wars. But before the coming of that time, the haughty and the mighty will be humbled. People will discard their idols of silver and gold, and the Lord alone will be exalted. (Chapter 2)

A prophecy for Isaiah's time. Isaiah declares that Jerusalem's leaders have led her astray. Her people will fall by the sword, her leaders will be punished, and the Lord will wash away the sins of Zion. (Chapters 3 & 4).

The Lord's vineyard. In his prophetic vision, Isaiah sees a vineyard that the Lord planted with choice vines. He tended it with care, and He had hoped to produce fine grapes, but it yielded rotten ones. So now, Judea, what should the Lord do with His vineyard? He will no longer tend it, and it will become desolate and overgrown with thorns. The vineyard of the Lord, Isaiah says, is the House of Israel. God had hoped for Justice, but wickedness prevails. Woe to those who drink beer and wine from morning to night, and host lavish banquets but ignore the ways of the Lord. Therefore, God says, My people will be exiled, and the grave will open its gaping mouth. Man will be brought low, and the holy God will be sanctified with Justice. (Chapter 5)

The throne of God. In the year of King Uzziahu's death, Isaiah saw a vision of the Lord's throne. Fiery angels minister to Him, and one calls to the other, "Holy, holy, holy is the Lord of Hosts; the earth is filled with His presence." The prophet cried out that he is unworthy of such a vision, and his lips are unclean. But, in his vision, a fiery angel took a hot coal from the altar with a pair of tongs. He touched it to Isaiah's lips and declared him purified. Then the Lord asked who will speak for Him. and Isaiah said "Here I am; send me." (Chapter 6)

Aram and Israel threaten Judea. In the days of Ahaz king of Judea, King Retzin of Aram and Pekah king of Israel went to war against Jerusalem, and the people of Judea trembled greatly. On the Lord's command, Isaiah warned King Ahaz of a plot to overthrow him, and cautioned him not to fear those two kings and not to call upon Assyria for assistance. Their attack will fail, Isaiah said; and soon the Kingdom of Israel will be no more. Isaiah gave Ahaz a sign: the young woman will be pregnant and will give birth to a son; and before that son can choose good over evil, the lands of Aram and Israel will be abandoned. (Chapter 7)

The fall of Damascus and Samaria. Very soon, Isaiah declared, Assyria will conquer both Aram and Israel, and their capitals—Damascus and Samaria—will be laid waste. And, because Judea did not trust in the Lord but called upon Assyria for assistance, Assyria will sweep through Judea and imperil Jerusalem. (Chapter 8)

A prophecy regarding King Ahaz's son. A son has been born to Ahaz, and, Isaiah says, that son will sit on the throne of David. He will reign with justice and will return the people to worship the Lord. In his day, the yoke of Assyria will be broken, and God will name him Prince of Peace. (Chapter 9)

Assyria—God's instrument. Isaiah declares that Assyria is God's instrument to punish Samaria. But when Assyria has fulfilled that purpose, God will punish the pride of the Assyrian king. Judea will no longer serve Assyria, and the remnant of Jacob will return to God. (Chapter 10)

A future king. In his vision, the prophet foretells of a descendant of Jesse (King David's father) who will arise. He will be filled with the spirit of the Lord, with a spirit of wisdom, and with reverence of the Lord. He will administer justice and will punish the wicked, and nations will seek his counsel. The wolf will dwell with the lamb, and there will be no evil or corruption throughout his domain. The Lord will redeem His people, gathering the exiles of Israel and the scattered people of Judea from the four corners of the earth. On that day, God's people will give thanks to the Lord, and there will be great joy in Zion, because the Lord will be in their midst. (Chapters 11 & 12)

The fall of Babylonia. Isaiah prophesies the fall of Babylonia. And God will return the House of Jacob to their own land. (Chapters

13 & 14)

The fall of other kingdoms. Isaiah prophesies the fall of Philistia (14:29–32) and Moab (Chapters 15 & 16), and the destruction of Damascus (Chapter 17).

Return. Isaiah prophesies the return of Israelites from faraway lands. (Chapter 18)

Egypt and Nubia. Isaiah prophesies that Assyria will conquer Egypt and Cush (Nubia). (Chapters 19 & 20)

The fall of Babylonia and Arabia. Isaiah describes the terror that will prevail when the Medes will conquer Babylonia. And he prophesies the conquest of Kedar (Arabia). (Chapter 21)

The fall of Jerusalem. A prophecy of the future destruction and exile of Jerusalem and Judea, and how the Lord will lament the destruction of His nation. The people of Jerusalem have not heeded the Lord's warnings. They feast, and they say, "Eat and drink, for tomorrow we die." (Chapter 22).

Tyre. Isaiah prophesies the conquest and destruction of Tyre (Chapter 23) and describes the destruction of the Kingdom of Israel (Chapter 24).

The latter days. Isaiah prophesies that the Lord will punish the enemies of His people and will vanquish the nations that made war against Jerusalem (Chapter 25). There will be rejoicing in the land of Judea, Israel will rise again, and all the children of Israel lost in foreign lands will return to the land of Israel (Chapters 26 & 27).

The fall of the two kingdoms. The prophet now rebukes the people of his own time. The inhabitants of Samaria are intoxicated with wine and beer, and destruction will come upon them like a flood. Isaiah reprimands Judea for following the ways of Samaria and warns of the disaster that will follow. (Chapters 28 & 29)

Samaria calls upon Egypt. The Kingdom of Israel asked Egypt for protection against Assyria (see 2 Kings 17:4). But, God says, Egypt will not protect Samaria from destruction. And when Assyria attacks Judea, Jerusalem must trust in the Lord. The Lord will break Assyria's might. (Chapters 30 & 31)

Note that after the Kingdom of Israel was exiled, Isaiah uses the name "Israel" to refer to the nation comprising all the descendants of the patriarch Jacob. (However, only the people of the Kingdom of Judea remained in their land.)

A king's responsibility. Isaiah says that a king has a right to reign only if he administers justice. (Chapter 32)

The return to Zion. A prophecy about an unspecified time, when the Lord will punish the enemies of Zion with death and destruction. The desert will bloom, the people of Zion will return to their land, and sorrow and hardship will be banished. (Chapters 33–35)

The Assyrian siege of Jerusalem. When, in the fourteenth year of King Hezekiah, the Assyrian king Sennacherib attacked all the fortified cities of Judea, and the Assyrian army continued to advance against Jerusalem, Hezekiah feared greatly. But Isaiah reassured Hezekiah that the Assyrian army will withdraw, and the Assyrian king will return to Assyria, where he will die by the sword. Hezekiah prayed to the Lord, and Isaiah sent a message to Hezekiah saying that the Lord had heard his prayer and would protect Jerusalem. That night, an angel of the Lord struck down 185,000 Assyrian soldiers, and in the morning the remainder of the Assyrian army withdrew. King Sennacherib returned to Assyria; and subsequently, while he was worshiping in the temple of one of his gods, two of his sons assassinated him. Those two sons fled, and Esarhaddon—another one of Sennacherib's sons—succeeded him as king. (Chapters 36 & 37)

Hezekiah's illness. King Hezekiah became deathly ill. Isaiah told him he will not recover. But Hezekiah prayed to God, and God told Isaiah to tell the king that his prayer was accepted, and God will grant him fifteen more years of life. (38:1–8)

Hezekiah's recovery. A poem of thanksgiving that Hezekiah composed on recovering from his near-fatal illness. (38: 9–21)

Babylonian emissaries. The Babylonian king sent a present to Hezekiah to wish him well on his recovery, and Hezekiah gave the Babylonian emissaries a tour of the palace and treasury. The Lord sent Isaiah to the palace, and Isaiah told Hezekiah that because of Hezekiah's indiscretion, all the treasures in the palace will be carried away to Babylonia. Also, Isaiah said, some of Hezekiah's progeny will be made into eunuchs to serve in the Babylonian palace. But none of those events will come to pass during Hezekiah's lifetime. (Chapter 39)

Consolation, and return. God commands His prophets to console His people. God has not abandoned His nation, and He will bring them back to Zion. (Chapter 40)

The punishment of Israel's enemies. Isaiah prophesies that God will judge the nations that have opposed Israel—*i.e.* the descendants of Jacob—and have denied God's power. Isaiah tells his people not to be afraid, because the Lord is with them, and Israel's enemies will be vanquished. (Chapter 41)

Israel's redemption. God, the creator of man, will redeem Israel from exile and will punish Israel's enemies. Israel was exiled for being sinful, but they are still God's nation. The Lord says to

Israel, "Do not fear, because I am with you." He will gather His people from the east and from the west. He will redeem Israel, and He will erase Israel's sins; He will return them to their land, and aside from Him there is no redeemer. (Chapters 42 & 43)

A call to repentance. "And now," says the Lord, King of Israel, "I am the first, and I am the last." The Lord created heaven and earth, and He created the nation of Israel to fulfill His purpose. Isaiah calls on Israel to repent and return to the Lord. There will be a return to Zion, and the land of Judea will be rebuilt. (Chapter 44)

Cyrus, future king of Persia. A prophecy addressed to Cyrus. Even though Cyrus will have no knowledge of the Lord, the Lord will give him power to conquer other nations. But, the prophet says, God is the Lord, and there is none other except for Him. He forms light and creates darkness; He makes peace, and creates evil. He is the Lord, Who creates all. (Chapter 45)

The downfall of Babylon. Isaiah prophesies the fall of Babylon and the return of the Judean exiles to Jerusalem. (Chapters 46–48)

Isaiah's appointment as a prophet. Isaiah says that God chose him in the womb to be a prophet, and He made Isaiah's mouth like a sharp sword. (49:1–6)

The land of Israel will be rebuilt. God chose Israel as His nation, and Isaiah says that God has not forgotten Israel. He will bring His people back from far away, and they will rebuild the ruins of their land. (49:7–26)

A call to repentance. Isaiah declares that the Lord has not divorced His nation. God has sent His people away because of their sins, and the prophet exhorts the nation to return to the Lord. (Chapter 50)

A call to follow God's teachings. Isaiah urges the people to take an example from Abraham and Sarah, and they are to follow in the Lord's ways. Through their following God's words, they will re-establish their land, and the Lord will affirm, "You are My nation." (Chapter 51)

The restoration of Zion. This is a prophecy foretelling Jerusalem's rising from the dust. There will be peace and rejoicing when the Lord returns His presence to Zion. (52:1–12)

The despised nation. Isaiah sees a future time when Israel will rise to greatness and success. Isaiah envisions the nation of Israel as a man, whom he calls God's servant (as he also called Israel previously—see 41:8 & 44:1). The nations of the world find it hard to believe that this person, who has been despised and oppressed, and who has been considered to be afflicted by God, has now become so great. He has suffered the wounds that they inflicted on him. But, in that future time, God's righteous servant will bring others to righteousness, and he will receive his reward. (52:13 – 53:12)

The abandoned woman. Returning to the theme of Chapter 50, Isaiah likens Israel to a woman who is abandoned, but not divorced. And, Isaiah says, Israel will not remain forsaken forever. "In a flash of fury I hid my face from you a moment"; but, says the Lord, with great compassion He will gather Israel back, and Israel will dwell in peace. (Chapter 54)

Isaiah compares God's teachings to water. Just as the rain that falls from heaven causes the earth to bear fruit and sustenance for humankind, so do God's words transform people's nature and achieve God's purpose. (Chapter 55)

A prophecy regarding proselytes. Isaiah declares that any gentile who joins the nation of Israel and observes the Sabbath will be fully accepted among God's people; and when the Lord returns the scattered children of Israel to their land, the proselyte will also have a share among them. (Chapter 56)

Condemnation of heathen practices, and a call to repentance. Isaiah speaks against those who practice ritual fornication under fertile trees, sacrifice their children and pour libations to foreign deities; and he calls for repentance. The Lord will grant peace for those who return to Him as for those who were always near to Him; but there is no peace for the wicked. (Chapter 57)

Insincerity. A prophecy against those who fast insincerely, while continuing their wicked acts. Isaiah exhorts people to heart-felt observance of Sabbath and fast days. (Chapter 58)

Sin, and redemption. Isaiah says that sin is rampant, truth is absent, and there is no justice. But the day will come when the Lord will punish all His enemies, and redemption will come for Zion. (Chapter 59)

The return to Jerusalem. Isaiah describes the future joyous return to Jerusalem. The wealth of nations will flow to Israel. The children of your oppressors will bow down to you, and those who despised you will honor you. Israel will be mighty, and its people will inherit their land forever. (Chapters 60–62)

Edom. A prophecy foretelling the destruction of Edom. (63:1–6)

The new Jerusalem. Isaiah praises the Lord's compassion for His people, and he foresees the time when the Lord will rescue His nation from their oppressors. Israel rebelled against God, and God decreed their exile and destruction. But, Isaiah prophesies, the Lord will return His people to their land. He will devastate the nations that opposed Him. He will bring about a new world, and He will build a new Jerusalem. Israel will be reborn, and peace will reign throughout the world. (63:7 – 66:24)

JEREMIAH

God appoints the prophet. Jeremiah son of Hilkiah, a *kohen* from the territory of Benjamin, prophesied in Judea from the thirteenth year of Josiah king of Judea until the exile of Jerusalem. The Lord told Jeremiah that before Jeremiah came out of the womb, He had already appointed Jeremiah to be a prophet. He told Jeremiah to warn the people that, because of their sins, disaster will come from the north, and the enemy will attack Jerusalem and all the cities of Judea. (Jeremiah, Chapter 1)

Idolatry. God tells Jeremiah to reprimand the people of Jerusalem. Other nations do not abandon their gods, even though their gods are not gods at all; but Israel has abandoned the Lord, Who is the creator of life. The nation of Israel has worshipped foreign gods, and has called on Egypt and Assyria for assistance instead of having faith in the Lord. (Chapter 2)

Unfaithfulness, and return. Jeremiah compares idolatry to adultery, and he calls on Judea to repent and return to the Lord. He prophesies about the day when the Lord will return His people to their land. The people of Israel will return, and Israel will unite with Judea. (Chapter 3)

The coming invasion. Jeremiah complains to the Lord that, by tolerating false prophets, He has misled Jerusalem into believing that there is no danger. But very soon, the enemy will invade from the north. There will be war, and the land will be desolate.

(Chapter 4)

A warning. Jeremiah reprimands Judea for denying the Lord and worshiping foreign gods, for committing adultery and prostitution, and not believing the words of the prophets. Therefore, says Jeremiah, the Lord will soon bring a mighty nation from afar, to devastate the land and its people. But even then, God will not annihilate His people. (Chapter 5)

Insincere prayers. Jerusalem will be punished, Jeremiah declares: war will descend from the north. The nation's leaders have reassured the people, saying "Peace, peace"; but, says the prophet, there is no peace. People steal, murder, commit adultery, and worship Baal. Then they go to the Temple, they call to God, they bring Him sacrifices, and they think they will be spared. But, Jeremiah declares, God does not want their offerings. What He wants is that they listen to Him and follow in the path that He commanded them. Instead, says Jeremiah, they have ignored the words of the prophets and have built the Topheth in the Valley of Hinnom, where they burn their children in fire (as an offering to an idol). Therefore, the Temple will be destroyed, and Judea will be consumed. (Chapters 6–8)

Punishment of Judea and its neighbors. Jeremiah prophesies that Judea will be punished for its wickedness, and its people will be dispersed throughout the nations. But Judea's neighbors—Egypt, Edom, Ammon, and Moab—will also be punished for their sins. (Chapter 9)

Jeremiah's warning, and a prayer. Jeremiah warns his nation not to learn the ways of other nations and not to fear the omens of the heavens, but only to worship the Lord, Who is king of the world. Jeremiah foretells destruction, and Judea will be inhabited by jackals. He prays that God will punish Israel only in measured fashion but will pour out His wrath on the nations that have devoured His people and devastated the Temple. (Chapter 10)

God's covenant. The Lord urges the people of Judea to follow the covenant that He made with them when He took them out of Egypt. And Jeremiah prophesies God's punishment for the men of his own city—Anathoth—who tried to assassinate Jeremiah. (Chapter 11)

The return. Jeremiah asks God why wicked people prosper. God tells Jeremiah that the people of Judea will be exiled, but God will also exile Israel's enemies from their lands. And the day will come when the Lord will restore His people to their land. (Chapter 12)

Prophecy of hardships and exile. Jeremiah warns Judea not to listen to false prophets who say there will be no war or famine. God has decreed there will be drought, followed by war, famine, pestilence, and exile to a faraway land. But, God said, if the people return to Him, He will return to them. He will make them strong, and their enemies will not prevail against them. (Chapters 13–15)

A prophecy of exile and eventual return. Jeremiah foretells that soon Judea will be exiled. But the day will come when the Lord will bring His people back. And they will praise the Lord Who returned the people of Israel from all the lands to which they were scattered, and brought them back to their own land, which the Lord promised to their Patriarchs. (Chapter 16)

Idolatry and violation of the Sabbath. Jeremiah reprimands the people of Judea for idolatry, for violating the Sabbath day, and for putting their trust in people instead of in God. "Blessed is the man who trusts in the Lord." (Chapter 17)

The potter. God sends Jeremiah to a potter's shop to watch the potter work. When the clay pot that he was making came out wrong, the potter undid it and re-made it. Thus, says the Lord, Israel is in God's hands, and He will re-make Israel just as the potter molds the clay to his liking. (Chapter 18)

The broken jug. God sends Jeremiah to the Topheth in the Valley of Hinnom. There, Jeremiah breaks a jug and declares that God will break Jerusalem and all of Judea, because they have burnt their children in fire at the Topheth, as sacrifices to Baal. (Chapter 19)

Jeremiah's imprisonment. When Pashhur, the chief officer of the Temple, heard of Jeremiah's prophecy at the Topheth, he had Jeremiah beaten and imprisoned. When Jeremiah was later released from prison, he prophesied that Pashhur and his allies will be exiled to Babylon, and there they will die. (Chapter 20)

Zedekiah's request. When the Babylonians besieged Jerusalem, King Zedekiah sent messengers to Jeremiah asking him to pray to the Lord that the Chaldeans (*i.e.* the Babylonians) withdraw. But Jeremiah answered that God Himself will fight against Jerusalem. And, Jeremiah said that those who remain in the city will die, but whoever goes out and surrenders to the Chaldeans will live. (Chapter 21)

Prophecy to Jehoiakim. Jeremiah reminds the king of his duty to execute justice, and not to spill innocent blood. But, God says, because King Jehoiakim rules without justice, he will be killed, and his corpse will be dragged and discarded outside the gates of Jerusalem. (Chapter 22)

A Messianic prophecy. Jeremiah speaks against the kings who led the nation astray and caused exile, and he prophesies about the day when God will return His people to their land. At that time, a descendant of King David will reign, and justice will prevail.

(23:1–8)

False prophets. This is a prophecy against the false prophets and the people who believed those prophets' words and continued in their evil ways, both in Samaria and in Jerusalem. God sees everything that people do. His presence fills the heaven and the earth. (23:9–40)

The good, and the bad. The Lord told Jeremiah that those who were exiled with King Jechoniah (another name for Jehoiachin) will return to the Lord with all their hearts, and the Lord will return them to their land. But those who remained in Jerusalem—Zedekiah and his followers—will be punished for their evil with sword, famine, pestilence, and exile. (Chapter 24)

Prophecy about the exile. Jeremiah says that because the people of Judea did not heed all the warnings that God sent him to give them, now God will send Nebuchadnezzar king of Babylon to exile them. But, Jeremiah says, after seventy years the Lord will punish Nebuchadnezzar and his Chaldean nation for their sins, and Babylonia will be conquered and subjugated. "The Lord will roar from on high"; He will mourn for His Temple that is destroyed. (Chapter 25)

A mob attacks Jeremiah. God sent Jeremiah to prophecy in the Temple courtyard about the impending destruction of Jerusalem. As soon he finished speaking, a mob attacked him and wanted to kill him. They said there was precedent for killing a true prophet: King Jehoiakim had killed a man named Uriahu who was an acknowledged prophet of the Lord, for giving a prophecy similar to Jeremiah's. But a man named Ahikam son of Shaphan rescued Jeremiah from the mob. (Chapter 26)

Advice for Zedekiah. Jeremiah prophesied to Zedekiah and to five foreign kings who were allied with him, not to conspire against Babylonia but to submit to Babylonia's rule. (Chapter 27)

Hananiah the false prophet. A false prophet named Hananiah son of Azzur stood in front of Jeremiah and prophesied that the yoke of Babylon will be broken in two years. But Jeremiah declared that God had not sent Hananiah, and that Hananiah will die within that year. And so it was: two months later, Hananiah died. (Chapter 28)

Jeremiah's letter to the Judean exiles. Jeremiah sent a letter to the Judeans who were exiled to Babylonia with King Jechoniah (Jehoiachin). He told them to settle there, and to seek the welfare of the cities to which they have been exiled. They should not listen to false prophets who say they will soon return to Judea, because the exile will last seventy years. (Chapter 29)

A Messianic prophecy. God told Jeremiah that, after a time of great suffering, the day will come when the Lord will gather the exiles of Israel and Judea and will return them to the land that He promised to the Patriarchs. A voice is heard on high: Rachel weeps for her children and refuses to be consoled. But the day will come when there will be rejoicing in the land of Israel, because the Lord will rebuild His nation. He will re-establish His covenant with them, His Torah will enter their hearts, and they will all know the Lord. (Chapters 30 & 31)

Jeremiah buys a field. King Zedekiah imprisoned Jeremiah for prophesying that the Chaldeans will destroy Jerusalem and will capture Zedekiah. While Jeremiah was in prison, at God's command, Jeremiah bought a field in the city of Anathoth from his cousin Hanamel. In front of many people, he told his secretary Baruch to place the deed in an earthen vessel, to be stowed away for many years. Although the Chaldeans will soon burn down the city and exile its people, the Lord will return the people to their land. At that time, the Lord will make an eternal covenant with His nation. People will again purchase properties, and in the cities of Judea and the streets of Jerusalem there will again be heard the sound of mirth, the voice of a groom, the voice of a bride, and the voices of people thanking the Lord, for He is good. (Chapters 32 & 33)

A prophecy for Zedekiah. Jeremiah prophesies to the king that Nebuchadnezzar will conquer Jerusalem. Zedekiah will be captured, but he will not die by the sword. (34:1–7)

Hebrew slaves. At God's command, Jeremiah told all the people to release their Hebrew male and female slaves. (34:8–22)

Tradition. Jeremiah speaks about a certain family who, for close to 300 years have refrained from drinking wine and who live in tents. They continue their way of life, which is a family tradition. But Israel's traditions were not instituted by a person: they are God's commandments to His people. Therefore, all of Israel must adhere to those commandments. (Chapter 35)

The scroll of Jeremiah's prophecies. In the fourth year of King Jehoiakim, God commanded Jeremiah to write his prophecies in a scroll. So Jeremiah, who was then in prison, dictated his prophecies to his secretary Baruch. The following year, Baruch read the scroll to the people of Judea, and the scroll was brought to Jehoiakim. On hearing its words, Jehoiakim cut up the scroll and threw it into a fire. He ordered his men to bring Jeremiah and Baruch before him, but the Lord had concealed them. And Jeremiah again dictated his prophecies to Baruch, along with a new prophecy foretelling Jehoiakim's death. (Chapter 36)

The Chaldeans and the Egyptians. In the time of Zedekiah, the Chaldeans besieged Jerusalem. Pharaoh sent his army to assist Judea, and the Chaldeans withdrew. Jeremiah warned that Pharaoh's army would withdraw to Egypt, and the Chaldeans would return. Jeremiah left Jerusalem, to return home to the territory of Benjamin. But he was arrested, accused of trying to defect to the Chaldeans. He was beaten and put in a dungeon. After a long confinement there, Zedekiah called for Jeremiah and asked him what the Lord was telling him. The prophet answered that Zedekiah will fall into the hands of the Babylonian king. Jeremiah asked not to be sent back to the dungeon, and Zedekiah had him placed in a prison yard, with much better conditions. (Chapter 37)

Jeremiah is thrown into a pit. Jeremiah prophesied that whoever remains in Jerusalem will die by the sword, by famine, or by pestilence, and that the Babylonians will conquer the city. The ministers declared that Jeremiah's words were bad for morale. With the king's acquiescence, they lowered him into a muddy pit in the prison yard, and Jeremiah sank into the mud. But Ebed-Melekh the Nubian, one of the palace officers, appealed to the king, and the king sent Ebed-Melekh with thirty men to pull Jeremiah out of the pit. Zedekiah took Jeremiah aside and asked him for a prophecy, swearing that he would not have Jeremiah killed no matter what he will prophesy. Jeremiah advised the king to surrender to the Babylonians. And, he said, if Zedekiah doesn't do so, the city will be destroyed. Zedekiah ordered Jeremiah to keep that prophecy secret, and he did not surrender to the Babylonians. (Chapter 38)

The fall of Jerusalem. In the eleventh year of Zedekiah's reign, the Babylonians breached the city walls and burnt Jerusalem to the ground. Zedekiah had fled, but the Babylonians caught up with him. They killed his sons in front of him. They blinded Zedekiah and brought him in chains to Babylon. Meanwhile, Nebuzaradan, commander of the Babylonian king's guard, exiled most of the remaining people of Judea, but he didn't exile the poor. Nebuchadnezzar told Nebuzaradan not to harm Jeremiah. Nebuzaradan released Jeremiah from prison and gave him a choice of remaining in Judea or going to Babylon where Nebuzaradan would see to Jeremiah's welfare. Jeremiah chose to remain in Judea. (Chapter 39, and 40:1–6)

Gedaliah. Nebuchadnezzar appointed Gedaliah son of Ahikam son of Shaphan to be in charge of Judea. Johanan, one of Gedaliah's men, warned Gedaliah that the Ammonite king had hired a member of the Judean royal family named Ishmael son of Nethaniah to assassinate him. Johanan secretly asked permission to kill Ishmael; but Gedaliah didn't believe him, and he refused to permit it. Then, in the seventh month, Ishmael and ten henchmen killed Gedaliah and all the Judeans and Chaldeans who were with him. They also captured other Judeans, including the Judean king's wives whom the Chaldeans had not exiled, intending to bring them as captives to Ammon. But Johanan and his officers confronted Ishmael, and the captives were released. Ishmael fled to Ammon. (40:7 – 41:18)

Flight into Egypt. The officials and the people requested Jeremiah to ask God for directions. God told Jeremiah that the people must not run away to Egypt. If they remain in Judea (and are exiled to Babylonia), the king of Babylonia will later return them to their land; but if they go to Egypt, they will die by the sword, by famine, or by pestilence. When Jeremiah delivered God's warning, many accused him of prophesying falsely. They did not heed the warning. They went to Egypt, and they took Jeremiah with them. (Chapters 42 & 43)

A warning against idolatry. While in Egypt, Jeremiah prophesied to the Judeans who had fled to there, warning them not to sacrifice to idols. But the people did not obey, and they said they would continue to worship the Queen of Heaven. Jeremiah reaffirmed that disaster would overtake them in Egypt, and only few would live to return to Judea. (Chapter 44)

A prophecy to Baruch. Prior to the exile, in the fourth year of Jehoiakim king of Judea, God spoke to Jeremiah regarding his secretary Baruch. Baruch had wanted to become a prophet, but God said that Baruch will not become a prophet. (Chapter 45)

Egypt's defeat. Jeremiah prophesies Egypt's defeat in battle against the Babylonians at Carchemish by the Euphrates River, in the fourth year of Jehoiakim king of Judea, and a second defeat when the Babylonian king Nebuchadnezzar will attack Egypt, years later. (Chapter 46)

The defeat and destruction of other nations. Jeremiah foretells the fall of Philistia (Chapter 47), Moab (Chapter 48), Ammon, Edom, Damascus (capital of Aram), Elam, and other nations (Chapter 49).

The coming defeat of Babylon. Jeremiah prophesies that Babylon will be punished for destroying Jerusalem. A nation will come from the north and conquer Babylon. And the people of Israel will return to their land. (Chapters 50 & 51)

The last king of Judea. Chapter 52 retells the history of the last Judean king. Zedekiah was 21 years old when he became king. He rebelled against Babylonia, and Nebuchadnezzar came with his army and besieged Jerusalem. The Babylonians broke through the city walls, but Zedekiah and his officers had already escaped. After a pursuit northwards, the Babylonians captured Zedekiah and brought him before Nebuchadnezzar. Nebuchadnezzar killed Zedekiah's children before his eyes. Then he blinded Zedekiah, brought him in chains to Babylonia, and kept him there in prison until the day he died. In the nineteenth year of Nebuchadnezzar, on the tenth day of the fifth month, Nebuzaradan, commander of the Babylonian king's guard, destroyed Jerusalem and burnt the Temple to the ground. And the people of Judea were carried off to exile in Babylonia. Evill-Merodach succeeded Nebuchadnezzar as king of Babylonia. In the first year of his reign, the new Babylonian king released Jehoiachin (the next-to-last Judean king), after 37 years of imprisonment in Babylon. (Chapter 52)

EZEKIEL

The divine chariot. The book of Ezekiel begins about seven years before the destruction of Jerusalem, while Ezekiel son of Buzi the *kohen* was in exile in the land of the Chaldeans (*i.e.* Babylonia). God's spirit came upon him, the heavens opened up, and he experienced a divine vision. A storm-wind came from the north, with a large cloud and flashing fire. Within the cloud were four heavenly beings, each with four wings and four faces, and fire and lightning moved among them. There was a wheel next to each being, and the wheels moved with them, in whichever direction the divine Will impelled them. Above the heads of the beings there was a terrifying void; and above that, there was the appearance of a sapphire throne surrounded by a radiance, which was the Presence of the Lord. Ezekiel fell to the ground, and he heard a voice speaking to him. (Ezekiel, Chapter 1)

The Lord's message to Ezekiel. God told Ezekiel to deliver His message to the people and not to fear them. Whether the people heed his words or not, they will nevertheless know that a prophet was among them. Ezekiel saw a hand stretched out to him, holding a scroll upon which were written words of woe and lamentation. At God's direction, Ezekiel built a model of Jerusalem and prophesied about the coming siege of Jerusalem and the suffering of its people. (Chapters 2–4)

Prophecy of the destruction of Jerusalem. At God's direction,

Ezekiel set fire to the model that he had built; and he declared that, because Israel failed to adhere to God's laws and committed all sorts of abominations, death and destruction will ensue, and Jerusalem will be destroyed. A third of its people will die of pestilence and famine; a third will die by the sword; and a third will be scattered through the world. (Chapters 5–7)

The Lord's presence departs from Jerusalem. About a year after the vision described in Chapter 1, Ezekiel again had a vision of the four beings and the radiance above the heads of the beings, representing the Lord's Presence. In his vision, Ezekiel was transported to Jerusalem. The exile of Judea had not yet occurred, and Ezekiel witnessed the sinfulness and abominations committed in the city. Then, the four heavenly beings, the four wheels, and the Lord's presence rose into the air and departed Jerusalem, leaving the city to its fate. But, God said, the day will come when the Lord will gather all the people of Israel from the lands to which they were dispersed. The Lord will give them a new spirit, and they will follow in God's ways. (Chapters 8–11)

Prophecy about the exile. Ezekiel prophesied that the people of Judea will be exiled. The Judean king (Zedekiah) will also be taken to the land of the Chaldeans, and there he will die. People should not heed the false prophets who say that Jerusalem's destruction is in the far future: it is coming soon. Even if the most righteous of men—such as Noah, Daniel, and Job—now lived in Jerusalem, their presence wouldn't save the city. Only they would be saved, and the city would fall. When Jerusalem falls, God says, a small remnant will be spared. They will be God's people, and He will be their God. God will punish His nation for the sins they have committed; but in the end, they will be remorseful, and the Lord will forgive them. He will re-establish His covenant with them, and they will know that He is the Lord. (Chapters 12–16)

A parable about Zedekiah. God gave Ezekiel a prophecy in the form of a parable about a great eagle (representing Nebuchadnezzar), who took a seed from the land—Zedekiah—and planted it in Jerusalem (*i.e.* he appointed Zedekiah as king). Zedekiah flourished until he rebelled and violated his oath to Nebuchadnezzar. Consequently, Nebuchadnezzar will exile Zedekiah and destroy Jerusalem; but another descendant of the royal seed will arise in the exile and the Lord will bring him to Jerusalem. (Chapter 17)

A message to the wicked. God exhorts the wicked to rid themselves of their sins and create for themselves a new heart and a new spirit. (Chapter 18)

A lamentation. Ezekiel laments the fate of the sons of King Josiah. (Chapter 19)

A review of history, and a prophecy. In answer to some of the elders of Israel, Ezekiel recounts the history of Israel, God's expectations for His nation, Israel's rebelliousness against God's ways, and their desire to be like other nations. But even in exile, Israel is still God's nation, and someday He will bring them back to the land of Israel. (Chapter 20)

Punishment for sin. Ezekiel says that because of Jerusalem's sins—idolatry, bloodshed, incest and adultery, taking bribes, and dishonesty—God will bring the Babylonians to punish them; and just as Samaria was destroyed, Jerusalem will also be destroyed. (Chapters 21–23)

The siege of Jerusalem. Two years before the final destruction of Jerusalem, God told Ezekiel (who was in Babylonia) that the siege of Jerusalem had just begun. And God described the horrors of the siege to Ezekiel. (Chapter 24)

The fall of other kingdoms. Ezekiel prophesies about the coming fall of Judea's enemies who rejoiced at the defeat of Judea: Ammon, Moab, Edom, Philistia, and Tyre will all be vanquished and made desolate. (Chapters 25–27)

Tyre. God tells Ezekiel to reprimand the ruler of Tyre, who claims to be a god. When Tyre is conquered, the ruler will be killed. (Chapter 28)

Egypt. Ezekiel prophesies against Pharaoh, whom he calls the great crocodile of Egypt. Nebuchadnezzar will conquer Egypt, Nubia, and Egypt's other allies; and the cities of Egypt will be desolate. (Chapters 29–32)

The watchman. Just as a watchman warns the people when he sees an enemy coming, the prophet is a watchman who warns the people of Israel when they are doing wrong, so that they will change their ways. God says he doesn't want the death of the wicked, but He wants the wicked to repent and live. (Chapter 33)

The shepherd. The good shepherd cares for his flock; he does not care for himself and ignore his flock. The shepherds of Israel have neglected their flock. The Lord's sheep have been scattered and are prey to beasts. But the day will come when the Lord will gather his sheep from all the lands, and He will make with them a covenant of peace. He will bring them back to Israel and will be their God; and His servant David will be their shepherd. (Chapter 34)

The downfall of Edom. The prophet declares that because of Edom's lasting hatred of Israel, Edom will be conquered and laid waste. (Chapter 35)

Return to the land of Israel. God tells Ezekiel to prophesy about the land of Israel, which other nations have plundered and taken as their own inheritance. The time will come when the land will again bear its fruit for the people of Israel. The Lord will gather His people from all the lands to which they have been scattered and will bring them back to the land of Israel. He will give them a new heart and a new spirit, and He will purify them. (Chapter 36)

The dry bones. The spirit of the Lord came upon Ezekiel and transported him to a valley filled with dry bones. God told Ezekiel to prophesy to the bones and bring them to life. There was a great noise as the bones reassembled, and flesh grew upon them, but they were still not alive. At the Lord's command, Ezekiel prophesied to the wind, and the wind came from all directions, entering into the bodies. They came to life and stood upon their legs. God told Ezekiel that these represent the nation of Israel, which the Lord will lift out of their graves. He will breathe His spirit into them, He will return them to the land of Israel, and they will live on their land. The House of Israel and the House of Judea will unite and be one nation, the Lord's servant David will rule over them, and the Lord will place His presence among them. And the nations of the world will know that He is the Lord Who sanctifies Israel. (Chapter 37)

The war of Gog and Magog. Ezekiel describes the great war that will precede God's gathering of the people of Israel from among the nations and the return of Israel to their own land. (Chapters 38 & 39)

The rebuilt Temple. In the fourteenth year after the destruction of the Temple, Ezekiel had a vision in which the Lord transported him to the site of the Temple, and an angel showed him an image of the Temple rebuilt. The prophet describes the structure of the Temple and the worship conducted therein. (Chapters 40–46)

The land of Israel. Ezekiel describes the future borders of the land of Israel and the apportionment of the land among the twelve tribes. (Chapters 47 & 48)

HOSEA

Samaria's sins. Hosea son of Be'eri prophesied (in the northern kingdom of Israel) during the reign of Jeroboam son of Joash (*i.e* Jeroboam II) king of Israel. In Hosea's initial prophecy, the Lord commanded him to marry a prostitute, who symbolized Israel's going astray and deviating from God's commandments. He had children with her and gave the children names signifying the punishment that will befall Israel. (Hosea, Chapter 1)

Israel's return. Hosea says, the day will come that the children of Israel will be very numerous, and the Lord will gather the people of Israel and Judea together under one ruler. Israel has been like a wayward wife who has betrayed her husband. But the day will come that she will repent and return to God. In that day, the Lord will take her back and will betroth her forever, with righteousness and with justice, with love and with compassion. (Chapters 2 & 3)

A reprimand. Hosea admonishes the Kingdom of Israel for dishonesty, theft, murder, adultery, and idolatry; and he warns Judea not to follow on that path. The land of Ephraim will be laid waste; and, though Ephraim turned to Assyria for help, it will not avail them. (Chapters 4 & 5)

Punishment and healing. The prophet calls upon Israel to return to the Lord. For just as God punishes, He will heal. (Chapter 6)

Assyria and Egypt. Hosea admonishes Israel for asking Assyria and Egypt for help. (Chapter 7)

Prophecy of exile. Israel has forgotten its Creator. Therefore, Israel will be exiled and will wander among the nations. (Chapters 8–13)

A call for repentance. Israel is guilty of grievous sins. But, says Hosea, if Israel repents and returns to the Lord, God will take them back, and the nation of Israel will bloom again. Whoever is wise will understand this; whoever is insightful will know. "The ways of the Lord are straight; the righteous will follow them, but the wicked will stumble upon them." (Chapter 14)

JOEL

The Day of the Lord. The word of the Lord came to Joel son of Pethuel. A plague of locusts is coming: a mighty nation that will sow destruction and desolation on the land. Blow a *shofar* in Zion, says the prophet. Repent, because the Day of the Lord is near. It is a day of darkness, a day on which a mighty nation will come, spreading out over the land. Fire will go before them, and a conflagration will follow them: a great nation assembled for war. Before them the earth will tremble and the heavens thunder; sun and moon will darken, and the stars will withdraw their light. And the Lord will raise His voice before His army, a vast force that will do His bidding. Indeed, the Day of the Lord is awesome and terrifying; and who can endure it? But, says the Lord, return to Me with fasting and with prayer, and I will have mercy. (Joel, Chapters 1 & 2).

The coming of redemption. The Lord tells His nation that in future times, He will pour his spirit upon His people: their sons and daughters will prophesy, and people will have dreams and visions. There will be signs and wonders in the heaven and the earth: blood and fire and pillars of smoke. The sun will darken, and the moon turn to blood before the coming of the great and terrifying Day of the Lord. But whoever calls upon the Lord will be saved. At that time, the Lord will restore Judea and Jerusalem. He will judge all the nations who have scattered His people throughout the world, and He will make war upon them. God will sit in judgement over the nations. The Lord will roar from Zion; His voice will come from Jerusalem; and heaven and earth will quake. Judea will remain forever, and Jerusalem throughout the generations. And all will know that the Lord dwells in Zion. (Chapters 3 & 4)

AMOS

The sins of nations, and the role of the prophet. These are the prophecies of Amos, who prophesied in the northern kingdom of Israel during the reign of Jeroboam son of Joash (*i.e* Jeroboam II) king of Israel. His prophecies began two years before the great earthquake (of 760 BCE). The prophet condemns Aram, Philistia, Tyre, Edom, Moab, and Ammon for their betrayal and grievous sins against Israel. And he condemns Judea and Samaria for abandoning the Torah and for doing injustice. God says to Israel, "I brought you up out of the land of Egypt and led you through the desert for forty years"; and I gave you prophets to direct you. But Israel commanded the prophets not to prophesy. God sends His prophets to warn His people before He acts. "If a lion roars, who will not fear? If the Lord God speaks, who will not prophesy?" (Amos, Chapters 1–3)

Injustice and idolatry. God admonishes Israel for injustice and idolatry, and for these sins the kingdom of Israel will fall. God tells people to seek Him, and live. But He will not accept their meaningless sacrifices and their songs. What God wants is that they do justice and righteousness. (Chapters 4–6)

Amos's prophecy of destruction. Amos prophesies the destruction of the northern kingdom of Israel. The priest of Bethel (where the Golden Calf was worshipped) tells Amos to flee to Judea and not to prophesy in the north. But Amos answers that the king of Israel will die by the sword, and the priest will be exiled and will die in a foreign land. (Chapters 7 & 8)

Rebirth. Amos prophesies that after the exile, the day will come when the Lord will re-establish the fallen House of David, and He will restore it as in days of old. He will return the people of Israel to their land, and He will rebuild the ruins of their cities. He will plant them in their land, and they will never again be uprooted, says the Lord. (Chapters 8 & 9)

OBADIAH

Prophecy against Edom. The book of Obadiah consists of only one prophecy, in a single chapter. Obadiah prophesies the fall of Edom, because they have inflicted great harm upon Israel. And, as they have done, so it will be done to them.

JONAH

God sends Jonah to prophesy. God tells Jonah son of Amitai to go to the Assyrian city of Nineveh and prophesy to them to change their evil ways. Jonah doesn't want to go to Nineveh. Instead, he purchases a ticket to travel on a ship to Tarshish, a faraway land. God brings about a storm at sea, and the ship is in danger of sinking. Jonah knows that the storm is on his account, and he tells the captain that the storm will stop if the crew throws him overboard. At first, the captain refuses to do such a thing, but finally he sees he has no alternative or the ship will go down. Jonah is thrown overboard, and the sea immediately becomes quiet. God sends a big fish to swallow Jonah, and Jonah prays to God from within the belly of the fish. Jonah repents, and God has the fish regurgitate Jonah onto dry land. Jonah goes to Nineveh and delivers God's message: in forty days, Nineveh will be destroyed. The people of Nineveh repent, and God spares the city. Jonah is distressed, because God did not carry out His threat and because Nineveh did not receive the punishment it deserved. But God answers Jonah, how could He not have mercy for that city of more than 120,000 people? (Jonah, Chapters 1–4)

MICAH

The fall of Israel and Judea. The word of the Lord came to Micah during the reigns of Jotham, Ahaz, and Hezekiah, kings of Judea. Micah prophesied that the Lord will bring destruction and devastation both to Samaria and to Judea in punishment for their idolatry, injustice, and thievery. (Micah, Chapters 1–3)

Rebirth. Micah prophesies that in the latter days, all nations will flock to Zion, to learn God's ways and follow His teachings. They will beat their swords into ploughshares, and there will be no more wars. (This prophecy of Micah is similar to the second chapter of Isaiah.) (4:1–9)

But first, a war. Before the rebirth of Israel and the coming of a time of peace, many nations will gather against Zion, to punish her for her supposed guilt. But the Lord will save Israel from her oppressors, and Israel will crush her enemies. (4:10 – 5:14)

What does the Lord want of us? Micah laments his generation's lack of devotion to God's will. Israel must remember how the Lord brought them out of Egypt, and all that He did for Israel after that. And, asks the prophet, what does the Lord want from us? He doesn't demand animal sacrifices, nor does He want us to sacrifice our children. What the Lord demands is that we do justice and be merciful, and walk humbly with our God. (Chapter 6)

The final redemption. After Israel's devastation and exile, the Lord will lead His people back to their land, and He will show them wonders as He did when He brought them out of Egypt. God will forgive transgressions, He will exercise mercy, and He will cast all their sins into the depths of the sea. (Chapter 7)

NAHUM

A prophecy against Nineveh. The time of Nahum's prophecy is not stated. Nahum prophesies against the kingdom of Assyria and against Nineveh, a city of blood, fraud, and violence. Assyria will be conquered, and Nineveh will be destroyed. (Nahum, Chapters 1–3)

HABAKKUK

The might of the Chaldeans. The prophet Habakkuk complains to God, asking why God allows the wicked to flourish. And why does He let the Chaldeans become a great and mighty power and devastate the land? The Lord answers that the day of reckoning will arrive, at the appointed time. Meanwhile, the righteous person shall live by his faith. (Habakkuk, Chapters 1–3)

ZEPHANIAH

Destruction and rebirth. Zephaniah, who was the great-great-grandson of Hezekiah king of Judea, prophesied in the days of King Josiah. Zephaniah foretold the destruction of Jerusalem and the exile of its people. But destruction will also come to the surrounding nations that mock the exiles of Judea. And the day will come when the Lord will pour out His wrath upon the nations that have opposed His people. He will return His presence to Jerusalem, and He will return His people to their land. In that day, says the Lord, all nations will worship Him, and Israel will be revered and praised among the nations. (Zephaniah, Chapters 1–3)

HAGGAI

The Second Temple. In the second year of Darius (king of Persia, apparently Darius I), the prophet Haggai spoke the word of the Lord to Zerubbabel, governor of Judea, and to Joshua the high priest. The people had not yet rebuilt the Temple, because they thought the designated time had not yet come. But, said Haggai, the poverty of the land and the scantiness of the crops are God's punishment for the people's failure to rebuild the Temple (since their return from Babylonian exile). Zerubbabel, Joshua the high priest, and all the people were moved by Haggai's words, and they began construction. Then, Haggai spoke to any who still remembered the First Temple in its glory. He assured them that the presence of the Lord will also be within the rebuilt Temple, and its glory will be even greater than the first. (Haggai, Chapters 1 & 2)

ZECHARIAH

A call to repentance. In the second year of King Darius (presumably Darius I), the word of the Lord came to Zechariah, grandson of the prophet Iddo. God said to His nation, "Return to Me, and I will return to you." Zechariah saw a vision of a man riding on a red horse. He asked what that vision meant, and an angel said the vision represented the avenger that God sent to roam the earth. God had been somewhat angry with His nation, but other nations have inflicted great harm upon Judea. And now, the Lord will return with mercy to Jerusalem. (Zechariah, Chapter 1)

Redemption. In a vision, Zechariah sees an angel measuring Jerusalem. Another angel declares that Jerusalem will someday have a large population and will be unwalled. The Lord will gather His people from the four corners of the earth. He will bring them back to Zion, and His presence will dwell in their midst. (Chapter 2)

The vision of the Menorah. Zechariah is shown a vision of Joshua the high priest, and Satan is standing to Joshua's right, to accuse him. The Lord rebukes Satan. An angel commands that the nation's sin be removed and that Joshua be dressed in new, clean garments. The prophet sees a golden Menorah with its oil reservoir and its seven branches; and there are two olive trees, one at each side of the Menorah. The angel tells Zechariah that this is a sign the Lord will be with Zerubbabel (the governor of Judea) and will enable him to rebuild the Temple. The Lord will thwart the enemies who have prevented construction. Not by arms and not by might will it be done, but by God's spirit. And the two olive trees in the vision represent the two anointed Jewish leaders, Zerubbabel and Joshua. (Chapters 3 & 4)

The Temple rebuilt. Zechariah prophesies the re-establishment of Israel, with Joshua the high priest as its religious leader and a man called "the Branch" (apparently referring to Zerubbabel) as its ruler who will rebuild the Temple. (Chapters 5 & 6)

The restoration of Jerusalem. The Lord exiled His people and scattered them among the nations, because they did not keep His commandments; but the day will come when He will return His people to Zion. Jerusalem will be called the city of truth, and the mountain of the Lord. Just as the Jewish people were considered a curse among the nations, the house of Israel and the house of Judah will then be a blessing. And many people from among the nations will approach a Jewish person and ask to follow him, because they heard that the Lord is with the Jewish people. (Chapters 7 & 8)

A Messianic prophecy. Zechariah prophesies that Israel's king will come to Zion—a humble person riding on a donkey. He will abolish war and will make peace among the nations. (Chapter 9)

War. But before the Messianic age, at an undefined time, Zechariah prophesies wars, with the defeat of Philistia, Assyria, Egypt, and Lebanon. (Chapters 10 & 11)

And the final war, before the Messianic era. The nations of the world will gather together to make war against Jerusalem, and the city will be captured. But God will wage war against the nations.

The Mount of Olives—which faces Jerusalem—will be split in two. And the people will flee as they did in the earthquake at the time of Uzziahu king of Judea. That day will be dark; it will be neither day nor night, but towards evening there will be light. Then, the Lord will be king over all the earth. On that day, the Lord will be one, and His name will be One. (Chapters 12–14)

MALACHI

The prophet rebukes the people. The Lord says He has loved the nation of Israel, but they have not reciprocated that love. Malachi rebukes the people for profaning the sacrifices and for marrying pagan women. (Malachi, Chapters 1 & 2)

Punishment of the wicked. The day will come—burning like a furnace—when the wicked will be consumed, and mercy will shine upon those who revere God's name. Now, God tells His people to remember the Torah of Moses and keep its laws. And prophecy will resume when God sends the prophet Elijah before the coming of the great and terrifying Day of the Lord. (Chapter 3)

THE WRITINGS

PSALMS (*Tehillim*)

* The psalms indicated by asterisks are the most noteworthy psalms.

Ch 1.* An exhortation not to follow the ways of the wicked, but to live according to the path of righteousness and to study Torah daily, day and night.

Ch 2. A warning to rulers and nations not to think they can subvert God's plans.

Ch 3. King David's song of praise to God for being David's protector when David's son Absalom rebelled against him.

Ch 4. David cautions against following the path of sinners. And he urges that when people go to bed, they should contemplate their actions and behavior.

Ch 5. A prayer that God will punish the wicked, that He will bless the righteous, and they will rejoice.

Ch 6.* David prays to the Lord to cure his illness and restore his health. He is overcome by fear. He asks for God's mercy, to be saved from death.

Ch 7. A caution not to rejoice when God punishes your enemy.

Ch 8.* God is master of the universe, of the heavens and of wondrous creations. And yet, He has given seemingly-insignificant humankind dominion over the earth, the skies, and the seas!

Ch 9. This psalm, composed upon the death of Laben (perhaps David's son), says that God judges the world justly.

Ch 10. The wicked take pride in their success and assert that God pays no mind to people's actions. But God does in fact pay attention. He listens to the prayers of the humble, and He helps the weak and downtrodden.

Ch 11. The wicked try to undermine the efforts of the righteous. But the Lord watches over humankind, and He loves the righteous.

Ch 12. David prays that the Lord will protect the righteous against the lies and malicious words that the wicked speak against them.

Chs 13, 38-39, 86. David's prayers asking God to help him when he was in distress.

Ch 14. The enemies of Israel deny God's existence and think they won't be punished. They devour Israel. But God sees.

Ch 15.* David lists the qualities that make a person holy: one whose actions are righteous, who is honest in his heart, who refrains from slander, has not harmed others, and has not accepted a bribe..

Ch 16. I have set the Lord before me always, and I shall not stumble.

Ch 17. David asks God to hear his prayer, examine his soul, and protect him against his enemies.

Ch 18. A song that David sang thanking God for saving him from his enemies and from Saul.

Ch 19.* The heavens proclaim God's glory, and all of creation speaks His greatness. The Lord's Torah restores the soul and imparts wisdom.

Ch 20.* It is not through military might but by the Lord's support that Israel will prevail. May the Lord answer when we call!

Ch 21. The righteous thank God for what they have. The wicked will burn as in a furnace.

Ch 22. Enemies rejoice at Israel's downfall. But God hears our prayers, and He is king over all the nations.

Ch 23.* The Lord is my shepherd, and He guides me through the darkest valleys. He restores my spirit, and I fear no harm, because He is with me.

Ch 24.* All the earth is the Lord's.

Chs 25–26. The quest for self-improvement, righteousness, and purity of heart.

Ch 27.* David expresses trust in the Lord's protection against his enemies. And he asks to dwell in the Lord's Presence all the days of his life.

Chs 28–29*. David proclaims that the Lord is his rock, his strength, and his shield. He prays that the Lord will continue to guide and elevate him and his nation, that the Lord will give His nation strength, and will bless His nation with peace.

Ch 30. A song that David composed, to be sung at the inauguration of the Temple.

Ch 31. A song of trust in God. David proclaims that the Lord is his fortress, and in His hand he entrusts his spirit. The Lord is his redeemer, Who has been merciful to him.

Ch 32. An exhortation for sinners to repent.

Ch 33.* The righteous should be especially grateful to the Lord. The Lord sees all mankind, and His eye is directed to those who revere Him and hope for His mercy.

Ch 34. David's prayer of thanks to the Lord for saving him from danger.

Ch 35. David's prayer requesting that the Lord save him from future enemies and dangers.

Chs 36–37. The wicked person is seduced by evil. He plots against the righteous, but his day will come. The righteous must trust in the Lord.

Ch 40. Happy is the person who puts his trust in the Lord. God does not want burnt offerings; He wants people to do His will and follow His teachings.

Ch 41. David's prayer to God to save him from his enemies and from illness.

Ch 42. The soul thirsts for God, the source of life.

Ch 43. A prayer to be saved from treacherous people.

Chs 44–46, 83. Prayers asking God to fight the enemies and the oppressors of Israel.

Chs 47*–48. All nations will rejoice when God will be king over all the earth, and He will reign from Zion.

Ch 49. Both the rich and the poor end up in the grave, but God redeems the soul from the grave.

Ch 50. A reprimand of those who reject God's teachings.

Ch 51. King David's prayer asking God to forgive him for sinning with Bathsheba.

Ch 52. David's response to Doeg the Edomite's slandering him to King Saul. (See 1 Samuel, chapter 22.)

Ch 53. The Godless attack and devour God's nation. But God will save His people from their foes, and Israel will triumph over its enemies.

Ch 54. A prayer asking God to save from their enemies all those who trust in Him.

Ch 55. David curses the enemies who tried to have him killed.

Chs 56–57, 59, 61, 63. David's prayers to God when King Saul sought to kill him, and when he was fleeing from King Saul.

Ch 58. A prayer for God to save the righteous person from his evil enemies.

Ch 60. David's prayer when he fought against Aram and Edom (see

2 Samuel, chapter 8).

Ch 62. God is King David's source of strength, in Whom he trusts to deliver him from hardship and from his enemies.

Chs 64, 70–71. David's prayers to God to save him from his enemies.

Chs 65–67. All of mankind comes to God in prayer, and He forgives their sins.

Chs 68–69, 108. David's prayers asking God to fight the enemies and the oppressors of Israel.

Ch 72. David's prayer about his son Solomon, asking that he be a just king who will reign in peace and will be revered by other nations.

Ch 73. David tries to understand why evil men prosper.

Ch 74. David questions why God, Who is all-powerful, allows Israel's enemies to devastate and oppress His nation; and David asks God to look to the covenant.

Ch 75. A song of praise to the Lord for His wondrous deeds.

Ch 76. A song of praise to the Lord for Israel's stunning military victory over an enemy.

Ch 77. A prayer for God to help His nation Israel in its troubles through the ages.

Ch 78. David summarizes Israel's history up to the start of his reign, and he praises God's wondrous deeds on behalf of Israel despite Israel's frequent lack of faith and sinfulness. But God is merciful and forgives sins.

Ch 79.* Foreign nations have entered Israel, defiled the holy Temple, and made Jerusalem into ruins. This psalm is a prayer asking God to pour out His wrath against the nations that have attacked and devoured Israel.

Ch 80. A prayer for God to restore Israel to His favor and to deliver Israel from its enemies.

Ch 81. God admonishes Israel for disregarding His teachings in spite of all He has done for them, and He urges them to follow in His ways.

Ch 82. God admonishes judges to judge the downtrodden fairly.

Ch 84. A psalm praising those who trust in the Lord.

Ch 85. A psalm asking God to restore Israel to His favor.

Ch 87. A psalm describing Zion as the city of God.

Ch 88. A prayer uttered while in great distress, asking to be saved from the grave.

Ch 89. The Lord, Who reigns over all creation, has selected David and his descendants to rule His nation. The nation celebrates the Lord, Who is their glory and strength. But if the people abandon His teachings and violate His commandments, God will punish the nation. Nevertheless, He will not dissolve His covenant with Israel, nor alter His promise.

Ch 90.* Moses's prayer contrasting the shortness of our lives with the eternity of God, and an exhortation for people to return to the Lord.

Ch 91.* A prayer asking God for protection from harm. Put your trust in the Lord, and He will be your refuge. He will charge His angels to guard you wherever you go.

Ch 92.* A song for the Sabbath day.

Ch 93.* The Lord reigns in majesty and might, over all the world. His kingship has existed through eternity.

Ch 94. The wicked commit murder and think that God doesn't see. But He will return their actions against them, and He will destroy them.

Chs 95–98.* Songs praising the Lord, Who created the world and rules it with justice. He has power over earth and sea. Israel is

His flock, and we proclaim His glory and His wondrous deeds among the nations.

Chs 99–100. The Lord is exalted in Zion, but He rules with justice over the entire world. All nations, praise the Lord, and worship Him with joy.

Ch 101. David wants to associate only with honest, kind-hearted, and humble people.

Ch 102. A prayer to be said when in great distress, when all is bleak.

Ch 103. David's prayer asking God to heal him from illness.

Ch 104. All of creation praises the Lord. May sinners disappear from the earth, and may evil be no more.

Chs 105–106. Psalms praising God for His covenant with the patriarchs and for all the wonders that He performed for His nation in Egypt and in the desert, so that they should follow His teachings. They sinned against Him; but He kept His covenant, and in His mercy He forgave them.

Ch 107. Those who have been saved from great danger should give thanks to the Lord.

Ch 109. David curses his enemies and requests God's help against them.

Ch 110. The Lord's power will radiate from Zion to vanquish His enemies.

Ch 111. A psalm of thanksgiving to God for His great deeds in fulfillment of His covenant with His nation.

Ch 112. A psalm in praise of the righteous person.

Ch 113.* A praise of God, Who raises the poor out of the dust and gives children to the childless woman.

Ch 114.* Nature itself trembled when God brought Israel out of Egypt.

Ch 115.* A psalm contrasting our God with the gods of the nations. Their gods have eyes but cannot see, and ears but cannot hear. But our God, Who is in heaven, can do whatever He desires. The heavens belong to the Lord, but He has given the earth to humankind.

Ch 116.* David's prayer thanking God for saving him from death.

Ch 117. All nations should praise the Lord for His mercy.

Ch 118.* All people should put their trust in the Lord.

Ch 119. A long psalm thanking God for His wonderful Torah, for His justice and His mercy, and asking God for His guidance in following His ways.

Ch 120. A psalm asking to be saved from those who speak falsehoods.

Ch 121.* A request for protection from the Guardian of Israel, Who neither sleeps nor dozes. He is our guardian, now and for all time.

Chs 122–125. Prayers for the welfare of Jerusalem and asking God to protect Israel from its enemies.

Ch 126.* When the Lord will return the exiles of Zion, it will seem as though in a dream. Those who sowed in tears will reap with joy.

Chs 127. A person's having children is compared to a warrior having arrows in his hands.

Ch 128. A psalm praising those who support themselves by the work of their hands.

Ch 129. Enemies have attacked Israel since her youth, but they have not overcome her.

Ch 130.* A psalm asking the Lord's forgiveness. If God kept account of all sins, who could survive? The Lord will redeem Israel from all of their sins.

Ch 131. David says he has not become haughty. He has put his trust in the Lord.

Chs 132–133. The Lord has chosen Zion to place His presence there. David and his descendants will continue to reign there, so long as they uphold the Lord's covenant.

Chs 134–135. Blessings for those who come to worship in the house of the Lord.

Ch 136. A psalm praising God for His creation of the world and for all the miracles that He performed when He brought Israel out of Egypt.

Ch 137.* On the rivers of Babylon, Israel mourns for Zion. If I forget you, Jerusalem, may my right hand lose its power, and may my tongue stick to my palate if I do not remember you. The psalmist asks the Lord to remember how the Edomites rejoiced at the fall of Jerusalem, and he prays that Babylon will be punished for the harm that they perpetrated on Israel.

Ch 138. David thanks the Lord, Who defends him in the face of his enemies.

Ch 139. God sees all. He sees what is in a person's heart, and He sees the baby in the womb.

Ch 140. David asks the Lord to protect him from evil men who plot against him and slander him.

Ch 141. David prays to God to help him resist speaking evil or doing evil.

Ch 142. David's prayer to God when he was hiding in the cave from King Saul.

Ch 143. David's prayer asking God to save him from his enemies.

Ch 144. David thanks the Lord for making him victorious in war.

Ch 145.* An alphabetical acrostic praising God, king of the universe. All the world should recognize both His might and His compassion. He supports those who are stumbling, and He provides sustenance for all His creations. He is close to all who call to him in earnest. He guards those who love Him, but He will annihilate the wicked. Everyone should praise the Lord and bless His holy name.

Ch 146. A psalm that presents a contrast between putting faith in human princes, who are limited, and putting one's faith in God, Who is all-powerful and eternal.

Ch 147. Israel has a unique place in the world: God gave His laws and His precepts to Israel, and not to any other nation.

Ch 148.* All of creation—heaven and earth, and all that is in them—gives praise to the Lord.

Ch 149. Let all of Israel rejoice in their Lord, Who gives them power to defeat their enemies.

Ch 150.* Give praise to the Lord, Who directs the world with His power and greatness. Praise Him with musical instruments. Let all living souls give praise to the Lord!

PROVERBS (*Mishlei*)

The acquisition of wisdom. This is the book of proverbs of Solomon son of David, King of Israel. He advises that reverence of the Lord is the foundation of knowledge. A person should listen to his parents' teaching and should resist the temptations of the wicked. The Lord gives a person wisdom, knowledge, and understanding, and enables him to be saved from evil men and from sexual temptation. (Proverbs, Chapters 1 & 2)

The fruits of trusting in God. Do not have an inflated opinion of your own wisdom. Trust in the Lord with all your heart, and do not depend on your own understanding. The Lord's teachings are like a tree of life for those who keep His commandments. Follow His teachings, and acquire wisdom; keep His commandments, and they will guard you. (Chapters 3 & 4)

Continuing in the straight path. Do not be misled to sexual impropriety, but rejoice in the wife of your youth. Do not follow the slothful and empty-headed; but take example from the ant, who works industriously although she has no taskmaster. Do not neglect your parents' teaching, nor forsake the Lord's commandments. For the Lord's commandments are like a lamp, and the Torah is a light to guide you and protect you. (Chapters 5–7)

The call of divine Wisdom. Wisdom calls to humankind: I speak truth, and all my words are just. Wisdom is better than precious gems, and superior to material wealth. Wisdom declares: through me rulers rule justly, and judges preside with righteousness. The Lord established me at the start of Creation, before all else was made. I was there when He made the heavens, and when He established the foundations of earth. (Chapter 8)

Do not try to rebuke a fool. If you rebuke a fool, he will hate you; and if you rebuke an evil person, you will be scorned. Give guidance to the wise person, and he will grow wiser. (Chapter 9)

A warning about loose speech. Excessive talking promotes transgression. He who spares his words is wise. (Chapter 10)

Contrasting the righteous and the wicked. Deceit in commerce is an abomination to the Lord. Honesty and integrity are pleasing to Him. Wealth will not protect from divine wrath, but righteousness saves from death. The actions of the virtuous elevate a city, but the speech of the wicked destroy it. (Chapter 11)

Additional contrasts. The purpose of the righteous is justice, but that of the wicked is deceit. A fool always believes his way is correct, but one who takes advice is wise. He who seeks out the wise becomes wiser, but he who follows fools comes to grief. A wise person is cautious and avoids evil, while the fool rushes in with confidence. (Chapters 12–14)

God sees the wicked and the righteous. The Lord's eyes are everywhere. He sees the wicked and the righteous, and people's hearts are open before Him. The Lord is distant from the wicked, but He listens to the prayers of the righteous. It is better to be righteous and have little than to have great earnings through injustice. A person may plan his life, but it is the Lord Who directs his path. Pride goes before destruction, and arrogance precedes a fall. (Chapters 15 & 16)

Proper behavior and social interactions. Grandchildren are the crown of the old, and the pride of children is their parents. He who seeks love overlooks wrongdoing; but he who continues a dispute turns away a friend. Starting a quarrel is like opening a dam; so before it breaks out, desist. A person should be sparing of his words; even a fool who keeps silent may be considered wise. (Chapter 17)

Various words of advice. It is foolish to give an answer before hearing an issue in full. The first to present his side seems correct, until the opposition examines him. Death and life are in the power of the tongue. Property and wealth are ancestral inheritance, but a wife with good sense is a gift of the Lord. Many are the thoughts in a person's mind, but it is the Lord's plan that will be accomplished. (Chapters 18 & 19)

Advice about accomplishing in life. Wine is a mocker, and beer is a rioter; whoever goes astray through them will not be wise. It is honorable to avoid a quarrel, but every fool will become entangled. Do not love sleep, lest you be impoverished; open your eyes, and you will have plenty. Ill-gotten bread may taste sweet; but later, the mouth is filled with grit. The soul of a person is a light of the Lord, revealing its innermost secrets. (Chapter 20)

Advice about being a good person. All a person's actions seem right in his eyes, but the Lord examines his heart. Doing right is more important to God than is giving Him an offering. Whoever stops up his ears to the cry of the unfortunate will not be answered when he is in need. Whoever guards his tongue keeps himself from trouble. (Chapter 21)

On wealth and lack thereof. A good reputation is more important than wealth. The rich are rulers to the poor, and a borrower is like a slave to the lender. Whoever sows injustice will harvest misfortune. The generous person will be blessed, because he gives bread to the poor. (Chapter 22)

Advice for living a good life. Apply your mind to discipline, and listen to words of wisdom. Do not withhold discipline from a child. Punishment may save him from the grave. Do not be an imbiber of wine or a glutton for meat. The wine flows smoothly, but later it bites like a snake: your eyes will see strange sights, and your mind will speak absurdities. Do not envy evil people, and do not desire to be among them. There is no future for the wicked; their doom befalls them suddenly. (Chapters 23–25)

Responding to disputes. Do not answer when a fool argues against you; but do answer him if your lack of response will cause him to think himself wise. Do not get involved in another person's quarrel, and do not be a quarrelsome person. (Chapter 26)

Do not be boastful. Do not boast about tomorrow, because you don't know what the day will bring. Let your praise come from others, and not from your own mouth. (Chapter 27)

How to handle errors. A person who covers up his wrongdoings will not succeed; but one who admits and renounces them will find mercy. (Chapter 28)

Contrasting behaviors. Various contrasts are made regarding the behaviors of the righteous and the wicked. (Chapter 29)

Putting trust in God. Who has gone up to heaven and come down? Who controls the wind, the waters, and the earth? All the words of God are pure, and they protect those who put their trust in Him. (Chapter 30)

The woman of valor. This last chapter is an alphabetic acrostic in praise of the ideal woman: a woman of strong character, wisdom, kindness, and moral strength. (Chapter 31)

THE BOOK OF JOB

The just and pious man. In the land of Utz, there lived a just and pious man named Job. He had seven sons and three daughters, and he was very rich. (Job 1:1–5)

Satan's complaint. All the angels come to report to the Lord, and Satan is among them. Satan complains to the Lord that Job is faithful to God only because God has blessed Job with everything. Just reverse his fortune, Satan says, and watch him change his tune! The Lord consents to allow Satan to test Job by any means, except that Satan may not harm Job himself. (1:6–12)

Satan tests Job. Job receives a report that all his children died when a roof collapsed; and soon after, he loses his entire fortune. In spite of his misfortune, Job does not rebel against the Lord. (1:13–22)

A more severe test. Satan asks the Lord for permission to harm Job, and see whether Job will still not curse God. God consents, on condition that Satan will not take Job's life. Satan strikes Job with severe illness, and he is covered with boils. Job's wife advises him to curse God and die, but Job will not do so. (2:1–10)

Job's three friends. Three friends come to Job to comfort him. Job curses the day of his birth. He can't understand why God is making him suffer when he has done nothing wrong. But still he doesn't blaspheme. (2:11 – 3:26)

The debate. Job's three friends tell Job to search his soul. Each presents arguments to show that surely Job must have done something for which he is being punished! But Job insists he has done nothing to deserved his fate, and he questions why the Lord would allow wicked men to prosper and righteous ones to suffer. (Chapters 4–31)

The fourth friend. After the three friends conclude their arguments and fail to convince Job, a fourth friend named Elihu speaks up. He summarizes the arguments of the other three friends and adds his own ideas. He says that the Lord often uses dreams and portents to give a person hints of his misdeeds, but sometimes the person fails to perceive the hint. An angel may then intercede, to rescue the person from death, and he is given two or three chances to correct his sins. God sees all and knows all, but His way of governing the world is beyond our understanding. (Chapters 32–37)

The Lord speaks to Job. The Lord reveals Himself to Job and speaks to him from out of a storm-wind. Why, God asks, does Job presume to understand what is far beyond his experience? Where was Job when God created the world and established the laws of nature? It is God Who created all that exists, and it is He Who gave people wisdom and understanding. But some things are beyond human understanding: God's wisdom is infinite, while man's is limited. (Chapters 38–41)

The conclusion. Job admits his limited understanding and submits to the Lord's wisdom. The Lord reprimands Job's friends who insisted that Job must have sinned. In fact, God says, Job was blameless. God blesses Job's latter days even more than his former ones. Job's former wealth is doubled, and he has seven sons and three daughters. Job lives to the age of 140 years and sees four generation of sons and grandsons. (Chapter 42)

THE SONG OF SONGS

A song of love. This book, composed by King Solomon, is a love duet between King Solomon and his lady love. It is filled with passion and words of love, with poetry and allegory. It was included in the Bible because it was seen as representing the love between God and the nation of Israel.

RUTH

Elimelekh and Naomi. In the days of the Judges, there was a famine in the land of Judea. A man named Elimelekh and his wife Naomi left the town of Bethlehem in Judea with their two sons and went to Moab, where there was food. Soon after arriving in Moab, Elimelekh died. (Ruth, 1:1–3)

The Moabite wives. The two sons married Moabite women named Orpah and Ruth. After about ten years in Moab, both of Naomi's sons died. Naomi decided to return to Judea. (1:4–6)

Naomi returns to Bethlehem. Both daughters-in-law accompanied Naomi to the border. Naomi told them to turn back, because there would be no future for them in the land of Judea. Orpah returned home, but Ruth remained committed to be a member of the Jewish people, and she refused to leave Naomi. They arrived in Bethlehem at the start of the barley harvest. (1:7–22)

Boaz. Naomi and Ruth were destitute, and Ruth went to glean grain in the fields. Most of Naomi's family wanted nothing to do with Ruth; but one relative, a landowner named Boaz, treated her kindly. Ruth gleaned grain in Boaz's field, and Boaz took a liking to her. Boaz wanted to marry Ruth, but there was a "redeeming kinsman"—*i.e.* a close relative of a childless woman's deceased husband, who was duty-bound to marry her—and that kinsman had priority over Boaz. (Chapters 2 & 3)

The marriage. As anticipated, the other redeemer refused to marry Ruth. Boaz then married her, and their great-grandchild was King David. (Chapter 4)

LAMENTATIONS (*Eicha*)

This is a book lamenting the destruction of Jerusalem and of the Holy Temple by the Babylonian king Nebuchadnezzar, and the exile of the people of Judea to Babylonia. The book ends with a request that God should restore His nation to be again as in days of old.

ECCLESIASTES (*Kohelet*)

All is transient. This book is an inquiry into the purpose of human existence, and what a person should value in his life. It starts with the premise that life is fleeting. Moreover, all that a person may do in his life has already been done before, and "there is nothing new under the sun." The author, who was a king in Jerusalem, says he made great effort to accumulate knowledge; he amassed great wealth and enjoyed all the pleasures and luxuries that life has to offer. And, he asks, is there any lasting value of these things, since in the end everybody dies?

The author's conclusions. A person should be happy and should do good in his lifetime, for a person's finding satisfaction in his activities is a gift of God. A man should enjoy life with a wife whom he loves, for that is what makes life sweet. A person should do all that he is capable of doing. One who waits for the right conditions will accomplish nothing. Life is sweet, and a person should find pleasure in all his days, even knowing that life is fleeting. Follow the desires of your heart, but know that God will judge you on all your actions. In the end, what matters is to obey God and keep His commandments, because that is the entire purpose of mankind.

Memorable quotes:

"All is fleeting." (1:2)

"That which has been is what will be, and that which was done is what will be done; nothing is new under the sun." (1:9)

"For everything there is a time, and a season for all things under the heavens." (3:1)

"All goes to the same place: all comes from the earth, and all returns to the earth." (3:20)

"A lover of money will not have his fill of money." (5:9)

"Wisdom gives life to its owner." (7:12)

"A live dog is better than a dead lion." (9:4)

"The race is not won by the swift, nor the battle by the mighty, … for time and chance overtake them all." (9:11)

"Quietly spoken words of the wise are heard better than the screams of the king of fools." (9:17)

"Even in your thoughts, do not curse a king; and even in your bedchamber, do not curse a rich person; because a bird of the sky will carry your voice, and a winged creature will report your words." (10:20)

ESTHER

The king's banquet. Ahasuerus, king of Persia, held a banquet in the capital city of Shushan (Susa) for all high officials of Persia and Media. He ordered his wife Vashti to come and show off her beauty, but Vashti refused to come. (Esther, 1:1–12)

Vashti's demotion. Ahasuerus took away Vashti's status as his queen, and, on the advice of his ministers, he held a contest to select a new queen. All beautiful virgins in his kingdom were invited to compete, and all of the contestants were kept in the palace for months of preparation for their presentation to the king. (1:13–22, 2:1–4 & 12–14)

Mordecai and Esther. In the city of Shushan there lived a Jew—*i.e.* a Judean—named Mordecai, who had been exiled from Jerusalem by Nebuchadnezzar king of Babylonia. His beautiful cousin Esther was an orphan, and Mordecai had brought her up as his daughter. When the king called for the contest to replace Vashti, Esther was taken to the palace as a contestant. (2:5–14)

Esther wins the contest. When Esther was presented to the king, the king fell in love with her, and he made her queen of Persia. But Mordecai had told her not to reveal that she was Jewish, and she kept the secret. (2:15–20)

Mordecai foils a plot on the king's life. Each day, Mordecai sat outside the palace waiting to receive a message from Esther. One day, Mordecai overheard two of the king's eunuchs, Bigthan and Teresh, plotting to kill the king. Mordecai told Esther, and she told the king in Mordecai's name. Mordecai's service to the king was recorded in the king's annals. (2:21–23)

Haman. Ahasuerus appointed a new prime minister named Haman, who was a descendant of Agag the Amalekite king (see 1 Samuel, Chapter 15). All the courtiers were expected to kneel to Haman, but Mordecai refused to kneel, and Haman became enraged. (3:1–7)

Haman's plot. Haman, after finding out that Mordecai was Jewish, resolved to kill not only Mordecai but all the Jews of Persia and Media. He paid the king a great sum of money, and the king approved Haman's plan and issued a decree to massacre all the Jews on a specific date that Haman had selected by drawing lots. (3:8–15)

Mordecai tells Esther she must intercede. Mordecai told Esther that it was her duty to plead with the king on behalf of the Jews, but Esther was afraid to do so, because even the queen was not allowed to approach the king unless he had called for her. If she were to attempt to do so and the king didn't indicate his approval by stretching out his scepter to her, she would be executed. Finally, Esther agreed to go to the king, but she asked Mordecai to have all the Jews of Shushan fast and pray for her. (Chapter 4)

Esther goes to the king. Esther put on her finest royal garments and approached the king. Ahasuerus stretched out his scepter to her and asked her what she desired. She responded by inviting the king and Haman to a private party on the following day, saying that then she will tell the king what she desires. (5:1–8)

Haman and Mordecai. Haman left the palace elated at the honor of being invited to a private royal party, but on his way home he encountered Mordecai and became enraged at the sight of him. When he got home and told his family, his wife Zeresh advised him to construct a gallows and on the morrow to ask the king to have Mordecai hanged. Haman was thrilled with that suggestion, and he constructed the gallows. (5:9–14)

The king remembers Mordecai. That night, the king had trouble sleeping. He got up in the middle of the night and asked that his annals be read to him; and by chance, the section about Mordecai saving the king's life was read. Upon inquiring whether Mordecai had ever been rewarded for his service and being informed that he had not, the king resolved to reward him the next day. (6:1–3)

Mordecai's reward. When Haman arrived at the palace, before he managed to ask the king to have Mordecai hanged, Ahasuerus asked Haman what he thought should be done to reward somebody whom the king would want to honor. Haman, thinking that Ahasuerus meant to honor him, suggested that the person to be honored should be paraded through the streets dressed in the king's garments and riding on the king's horse. The king ordered Haman to do exactly that to Mordecai. Haman did as he was ordered and returned home dejected. (6:4–14)

Esther's party. At Esther's party, the king again asked Esther what she desired. In response, Esther said she was pleading for her life and the life of her people, because a certain person planned to murder them. The king asked who would dare to do such a thing, whereupon Esther pointed to Haman. She revealed that she was Jewish and declared that Haman intended to murder her and all her people. Haman tried to plead with Esther, but the king, in a drunken rage, sentenced Haman to death, and Haman was hanged on the gallows that he had prepared for Mordecai. (Chapter 7)

The aftermath. Ahasuerus said that since all royal decrees were irreversible, he could not rescind his decree to massacre the Jews on the date specified. So instead, he issued a new decree authorizing the Jews to take up arms and defend themselves against their enemies on that date. Thus, on the appointed date, the thirteenth day of the month of Adar, the Jews of Persia killed many who sought their lives, and they declared the following day to be a day of celebration, which later became known as the holiday of Purim. Ahasuerus continued to reign, and he appointed Mordecai as viceroy. (Chapters 8–10)

DANIEL

The king's decree. The Babylonian king Nebuchadnezzar conquered Judea and exiled the Judean royal family and many of the prominent citizens of Jerusalem to Babylonia (see 2 Kings 23:36 – 24:16). Nebuchadnezzar had several of the captive sons of the Judean royal family and the Judean nobility selected to be trained in the language and culture of the Chaldeans (Babylonians). Among those selected were Daniel, Hananiah, Mishael, and Azariah, and they were given Chaldean names: Belteshazzar, Shadrach, Meshach, and Abed-nego, respectively. These four refused to be defiled by eating the king's food or drinking the king's wine, so the chief officer served them grains and water instead. (Daniel 1:1–16)

The boys are presented to the king. God conferred special wisdom and understanding on Daniel, Hananiah, Mishael, and Azariah. And so, when their training was completed and they were presented to the king, he found them to be wiser than all the other boys, and also much wiser than any of his sorcerers and counselors. He appointed them as his advisers, and Daniel continued to serve until the first year of King Cyrus. (1:17–21)

Nebuchadnezzar's dream. In the second year of his reign, Nebuchadnezzar had a dream that troubled him greatly, and he called his wise men to interpret it. But he refused to tell them the dream, because then he would have no way of knowing whether they were interpreting correctly. If they were really wise, the king demanded, they must tell him the dream and interpret it for him. When they were unable to do so, Nebuchadnezzar decreed that all his wise men be executed, including Daniel and his friends. Daniel requested a one-day stay of execution, and that was granted. Daniel and his three friends prayed for God's help. (2:1–18)

The dream is interpreted. That night, God revealed to Daniel the king's dream and its interpretation. It was a dream about a great statue composed of sections of gold, silver, bronze, and iron, representing four future kingdoms that will rule the earth. In the morning, Daniel went to the king and told him all. The king was satisfied, and he declared that God must be the God of gods. He gave Daniel great honor and appointed him to a high position in his court. (2:19–49)

The furnace. Nebuchadnezzar had a statue made of gold sixty cubits high, and he commanded that all people bow to the statue. Daniel's three friends refused to do so, and certain Chaldeans reported to the king that three Jews—Shadrach, Meshach, and Abed-nego—had violated the king's command. Nebuchadnezzar flew into a rage, and he had the three of them thrown into a fiery furnace. But an angel saved them, and they emerged from the furnace unharmed. (Chapter 3)

Another dream. Nebuchadnezzar had another frightening dream. He saw a great and beautiful tree growing in the ground, but an angel commanded to cut it down, leaving only the stump and the roots. The angel told him that the birds and the beasts will flee from the fallen tree, and, the angel said, this will last for seven seasons. Daniel told the king that the tree represents Nebuchadnezzar himself. The king will lose his mind and will be driven from human society. He will behave like a beast and will eat grass for seven seasons, until he repents of his sins and acknowledges God as the ruler over all the world. The dream was fulfilled; and, as foretold, when Nebuchadnezzar repented and acknowledged God, his kingdom was restored to him. (Chapter 4)

Belshazzar's feast, and the fall of Babylon. King Belshazzar (of Babylonia) held a banquet for all his high officials. Under the influence of wine, he ordered that the gold and silver vessels that Nebuchadnezzar had plundered from the Temple in Jerusalem be brought. As he and his guests drank from the Temple vessels, the fingers of a human hand appeared and began to write on the wall. Nobody could read the writing, and Belshazzar became very frightened. Just then, the queen remembered that Nebuchadnezzar had an adviser named Daniel, who was very wise. So Daniel was brought, and he interpreted the writing: the Persians will soon conquer the kingdom. And, as foretold, later that night the Persians invaded Babylonia, and Belshazzar was assassinated. (Chapter 5)

The den of lions. When Darius the Mede became king (of Persia), he appointed Daniel as one of his ministers, and he considered making Daniel his chief minister. Other ministers and satraps became jealous, and they conspired against Daniel. They had Daniel convicted of a capital crime, and Daniel was thrown into a lions' den. Darius was very distressed, and he fasted until the following day. In the morning, he went to the lions' den and was surprised to find that Daniel had miraculously survived unscathed. Darius then had Daniel's accusers thrown into the lions' den, together with their wives and children; and the lions immediately killed them all. (Chapter 6)

More visions. Daniel had other visions: one about four beasts rising from the sea, representing the four kingdoms about which

Nebuchadnezzar had dreamt previously; a vision of the divine throne with a river of fire flowing before it; and other visions foretelling what will befall Persia and Greece. Daniel had an incomplete understanding of the meaning of his visions, and the angel Gabriel descended from heaven to help him understand. (Chapters 7 & 8)

Daniel's prayer. In the first year of Darius son of Ahasuerus, Daniel studied the prophecies of Jeremiah, and Daniel prayed fervently, asking God to forgive the nation of Israel for its sins that had led to the destruction of Jerusalem. (Chapter 9)

A vision of Israel's future. In the third year of King Cyrus of Persia, when Daniel was at the banks of the Tigris River with some other people, an angel dressed in linen, with eyes of fire, appeared to him in a vision. Daniel saw the vision, but the other people saw nothing; and yet, they became very fearful as the angel spoke to Daniel and told him what would befall his nation in the ensuing years. (Chapter 10)

Nations at war. The angel told Daniel about the nations that will rise and fall, and of the rulers and the wars that will ensue over many years to come. (11:1–39)

A prophecy of the far future. The angel told Daniel about events that will occur in the far future, and the wars that will rage at that time. It will be a time of great distress for Daniel's nation, but the great angel Michael will stand as the guardian of Israel. Many of those who sleep in the earth will awaken as the final redemption unfolds. Daniel asked when it will be, and the angel gave him a cryptic answer that Daniel said he didn't understand. But the angel assured him that although the meaning of his answer is sealed for now, when the time arrives, his words will become clear. (11:40 – 12:13)

EZRA

The king's proclamation. In the first year of Cyrus king of Persia (*i.e.* Cyrus II, known as "Cyrus the Great"), Cyrus issued a proclamation allowing the Judean exiles in Babylonia to return to Judea and rebuild their Temple in Jerusalem. Cyrus also released all the gold and silver vessels that Nebuchadnezzar had taken from the Temple, to bring those vessels back to Jerusalem with the returning exiles. The returning exiles numbered 42,360, plus slaves and livestock. Their leader was Zerubbabel (a descendant of King Jehoiachin of Judea). (Ezra, Chapters 1–3)

The enemies conspire to thwart rebuilding the Temple. The enemies of the returning Judeans asked Zerubbabel to let them participate in building the Temple, but the leaders of Israel declined to allow them to participate. And so, all during the remaining years of Cyrus's reign, those enemies tried to obstruct the rebuilding of the Temple. They drew up an accusation against the inhabitants of Judea and Jerusalem, claiming that the Jews (*i.e.* the Judeans) were building a rebellious city and that they would pay no taxes. The Persian king was persuaded, and he ordered the building to stop. Building was not resumed until the second year of Darius's reign. (Chapter 4).

Building resumes. Inspired by the prophets Haggai and Zechariah, Zerubbabel began rebuilding the Temple. The enemies of the Jews challenged the legality of building the Temple, and the Jews petitioned Darius (Darius I) to search the archives and find King Cyrus's original proclamation permitting them to rebuild the Temple. Darius had the archives searched. Cyrus's proclamation was found, and Darius ordered the building project to resume. The Temple was completed in the month of Adar in the sixth year of Darius's reign, and the Jews held a joyous celebration of the Passover holiday in the following month. (Chapters 5 & 6)

Ezra arrives. King Artaxerxes of Persia (Artaxerxes I), in the seventh year of his reign, sent Ezra the scribe to Jerusalem. Ezra, a *kohen* who was fluent in the Torah, arrived in Jerusalem with the king's authorization to govern Judea and Jerusalem according to the laws of God. (Chapters 7 & 8)

Renouncing intermarriage. Ezra found that many of the Jews who had returned to Judea had intermarried with the local populace and had adopted the abhorrent practices of the Canaanites. Ezra prayed to God, asking Him to forgive the people for their sins; and just as Ezra concluded his prayer, the leaders of the people came to him. They pledged to separate themselves from their foreign wives and to re-dedicate themselves to the service of God. And so they did. (Chapters 9 & 10)

NEHEMIAH

Nehemiah is sent to Jerusalem. In the twentieth year of the reign of King Artaxerxes (*i.e.* Artaxerxes I of Persia), Nehemiah, who was the king's cupbearer, received word that the Jews who had returned to Jerusalem were faring very badly, that the walls of the city were breached in places, and the city gates had been burnt down. As Nehemiah served the wine, the king noticed that Nehemiah appeared disturbed, and he asked Nehemiah about it. Nehemiah, although fearing greatly, told the king why he was distraught, and he asked the king to send him to Jerusalem. Artaxerxes agreed to send Nehemiah, asking him only to specify the date of his return. The king also gave Nehemiah letters granting him safe passage, and he sent with him an escort of army officers and cavalry. When Nehemiah arrived in Jerusalem, he set the people of Judea to work repairing the city's walls and its gates. (Nehemiah, Chapters 1–3)

Sanvallat. The enemies of the Jews, led by Sanvallat the Horian, conspired to attack the Jews who were rebuilding the walls of Jerusalem. But their plot was discovered, and Nehemiah stationed guards at the walls to defend the builders. From that time on, Nehemiah had half the workforce assigned to building while the other half stood guard with weapons and armor. (Chapters 4 & 5)

Attempts against Nehemiah. When Sanvallat learned that the Jews had rebuilt the walls of Jerusalem but the gates of the city had not yet been rebuilt, he tried to lure Nehemiah to a meeting outside of the city. But Nehemiah realized that Sanvallat meant to do him harm, and he repeatedly refused the meeting. Also, Sanvallat sent messages to Nehemiah accusing him of fomenting rebellion against Persia and of planning to become king of Judea. And false prophets in Jerusalem tried to lure Nehemiah into doing scandalous acts. But, despite all these attempts, no harm came to Nehemiah. The walls of Jerusalem were completed in 52 days, and the gates were rebuilt soon after. (Chapters 6 & 7)

Holiday celebration. On the first day of the seventh month (*i.e.* Rosh Hashana), the people assembled in Jerusalem, and Ezra the Scribe read to them from a scroll of the Torah. Then he bade them celebrate the festival, for the day is holy to the Lord. On the following day, he continued teaching the people the words of the Torah, and he told them to gather materials to make huts (*sukkot*) to celebrate the festival of Sukkot (beginning on the fifteenth day of that month). This the people did, and there was great rejoicing. (Chapter 8)

The people's pledge. On the 24th day of that month, the people again assembled. They invoked the Lord, Who had performed great wonders on behalf of the people of Israel since the time of Abraham and Who had given them the land of Israel; and they made a solemn pledge, which they put in writing, to observe all the laws of the Torah. (Chapters 9 & 10)

Settling the people of Judea. The leaders of the people settled in Jerusalem. The rest of the people drew lots to live in Jerusalem, while nine out of ten lived in the surrounding towns. (Chapters 11 & 12)

Nehemiah's absence from Jerusalem, and his return. Nehemiah went back to Artaxerxes in the 32nd year of his reign, but after a while, he asked the king for permission to return to Jerusalem. On his return, Nehemiah found multiple irregularities and infractions in the operation of the Temple, and various sinful practices that had become prevalent in his absence. Nehemiah purified the Temple and worked hard to rectify the wrongs that the people had committed. (Chapter 13)

CHRONICLES

The book of Chronicles, which is divided into two parts (1 Chronicles and 2 Chronicles), is a selected summary of the narrative portions of the Hebrew Bible. The first nine chapters of the first book of Chronicles are devoted to genealogy. Beginning with Chapter 10, the history of Israel is told, beginning with King Saul's war against the Philistines and continuing through David's reign. The second book of Chronicles begins with King Solomon's reign and continues through the exile of Judea by King Nebuchadnezzar of Babylonia, and the subsequent proclamation of King Cyrus of Persia about fifty years later, allowing the exiled Judeans—the Jews—to return to Jerusalem to rebuild the Temple. While the book of Chronicles is a retelling of the second book of Samuel and the book of Kings, it adds some significant details that were not previously presented. I have chosen to insert those details into my narrative of those books, and have referenced the location in the book of Chronicles where those additional details are found.

ACKNOWLEDGEMENTS

I want to thank my father Hillel Bavli, who inspired my love of the Hebrew Bible and gave me an intimate knowledge of and proficiency in Biblical Hebrew. My father, although mainly known as a Hebrew poet and Professor of Hebrew Literature, knew the entire Hebrew Bible by heart and taught Bible courses. He and my mother, Rahela Bavli—also a Hebrew poet—spoke to me only in Hebrew when I was little, thereby imparting to me a sensitivity to the nuances of the Hebrew language.

And above all, I thank the light of my life, my dear wife and soulmate Madeline, who helped me tremendously in editing this book.

ABOUT THE AUTHOR

Samuel Bavli is professionally trained as a medical doctor specializing in endocrinology. His father, the Hebrew poet Hillel Bavli, who had a prodigious knowledge of the Bible, instilled in him a love of the Hebrew Bible and a sensitivity to the nuances of Biblical Hebrew. Dr. Bavli is now retired from medicine, and he devotes much of his time to writing and to studying Torah. Over the course of many years, he has taught classes on Isaiah and other Biblical studies at the Orthodox synagogue where he is a member. His most recent book, *The Light of the Torah*, is a collection of essays discussing major concepts in the Torah. He is also the author of two books of historical fiction.

INDEX OF NAMES AND PLACES

Aaron 23, 24, 25, 26, 31, 32, 33, 35, 37, 38, 39, 44, 45, 46, 47, 48, 49, 50, 51, 52, 62

Abed-nego 196, 197

Abel 3

Abiathar 100

Abigail 101, 102

Abihu 33, 38, 44

Abijah 117

Abijam 117

Abimelekh 8, 9, 11, 84, 85

Abinadab 105

Abner 101, 103, 104, 112

Abraham xi, 7, 8, 9, 10, 11, 14, 141, 203

Abram 5, 6, 7

Absalom 107, 108, 109, 111, 173

Adam xi, 3, 4

Adoni-Bezek 81

Adonijah 111, 112

Agag 97, 193

Ahab 118, 119, 120, 121, 122, 123, 124

Ahasuerus xii, 192, 193, 194, 195, 199

Ahaz 127, 128, 129, 134, 135, 136, 165

Ahaziah 120, 121, 123, 124

Ahijah 115

Ahikam son of Shaphan 148, 152

Ahimelekh 99, 100

Ahinoam 101, 102

Ahithophel 108, 109

Ai 76, 77

Akhish 101, 102

Amalek 29, 67, 96

Amalekites 29, 82, 84, 97, 102

Amasa 109, 110, 112

Amaziah 125, 126

Amitai 164

Ammon 85, 95, 106, 145, 152, 153, 158, 163

Ammonite 66, 85, 107, 152

Ammonites 8, 82, 85, 95, 96

Amnon 107, 108

Amon 131

Amorite 52, 75, 76, 77, 78, 85

Amorites 52, 53, 78, 81

Amos 163, 164

Amotz 134

Anathoth 146, 149

Arabia 137

Arabians 123, 126

Arad 52

Aram 10, 53, 54, 81, 106, 117, 119, 120, 122, 123, 124, 125, 127, 128, 135, 136, 153, 163, 176

Aramean 106, 119, 120, 122, 123, 124, 125

Arameans 106, 119, 123

Artaxerxes xii, 201, 202, 204

211

Asa 117, 118, 120

Asenath 17

Ashdod 93

Asher 12

Asherah 117, 131

Ashkelon 87

Assyria xi, xviii, 127, 128, 129, 130, 132, 135, 136, 137, 138, 144, 161, 166, 169

Atalia 123, 124, 125

Avdon 86

Avihu 33

Avishag 111, 112

Azariah 196

Azariah, king, 126, 127

Baal xviii, 27, 54, 55, 83, 84, 85, 118, 119, 121, 124, 125, 128, 131, 145, 147

Baal-Peor 54, 55

Baal-Zevuv 121

Baasha 117, 118

Babylon 5, 132, 140, 147, 148, 149, 152, 153, 154, 181, 198

Babylonia xi, xii, xviii, 128, 130, 132, 133, 136, 137, 139, 148, 149, 152, 153, 154, 155, 157, 190, 192, 196, 198, 200, 205

Babylonians 147, 151, 152, 153, 154, 157, 196

Balaam 53, 54, 56

Balak 53, 54

Barak 82, 83

Baruch 149, 150, 153

Bathsheba 106, 107, 111, 112, 176

Bavel 5

Be'eri 161

Beer-Sheba 11, 19, 113

Belshazzar 198

Benaiah 112

Ben-Hadad 117, 119, 123

Benjamin xi, xviii, 14, 17, 18, 89, 90, 94, 110, 116, 144, 151

Ben-Oni 14

Bethel 14, 76, 116, 124, 132, 164

Bethlehem 86, 89, 97, 189

Beth-Shemesh 93

Bezalel 33, 35

Bezek 81

Bezer 60

Bigthan 192

Bil'am 53

Bilha 12

Boaz 189, 190

Buzi 155

Cain 3

Caleb 48, 49, 79, 81

Canaan xi, 5, 6, 7, 10, 12, 13, 15, 17, 18, 19, 20, 22, 29, 31, 35, 48, 57, 58, 65, 77, 78, 79, 80

Canaanite 31, 35, 40, 52, 63, 78, 80, 82, 114

Canaanites 10, 35, 39, 59, 60, 61, 62, 65, 75, 78, 80, 81, 201

Cave of Machpelah 10, 19

Chaldean 148, 196

Chaldeans 147, 149, 150, 151, 152, 155, 156, 166, 167, 196, 197

INDEX OF NAMES AND PLACES

Cush 137

Cushan-Rishatayim 81, 82

Cutha 128

Cyrus xii, 133, 140, 196, 199, 200, 201, 205

Dagon 89, 92, 93

Damascus 106, 119, 123, 126, 128, 136, 137, 153

Dan 12, 33, 86, 113, 116, 124

Daniel xix, 156, 196, 197, 198, 199

Darius xii, 167, 168, 198, 199, 200, 201

David xi, xvii, xviii, 97, 98, 99, 100, 101, 102, 103, 104, 105, 106, 107, 108, 109, 110, 111, 112, 113, 114, 115, 116, 136, 147, 158, 159, 164, 173, 174, 175, 176, 177, 178, 179, 180, 181, 183, 190, 205

Dead Sea 57, 78

Deborah xvii, 82, 83

Delilah 88

Dinah 12, 14

Doeg 99, 100, 176

Ebed-Melekh 151

Edom 15, 51, 52, 57, 59, 79, 105, 114, 122, 126, 142, 145, 153, 158, 163, 164, 176

Edomite 99, 100, 176

Edomites 14, 66, 96, 106, 128, 181

Eglon 82

Egypt xi, xvi, 5, 6, 7, 9, 11, 16, 17, 18, 19, 20, 21, 22, 23, 24, 25, 26, 27, 28, 29, 31, 33, 39, 41, 43, 44, 45, 46, 47, 48, 51, 57, 61, 62, 67, 69, 75, 80, 85, 93, 112, 113, 115, 116, 117, 128, 132, 137, 138, 144, 145, 146, 151, 152, 153, 158, 161, 163, 166, 169, 179, 181

Ehud xvii, 82

Ein-Gedi 100

Ekron 93, 121

Elah 118, 127, 128

Elam 6, 153

Eleazar 44, 52, 54, 55, 56

Eli 91, 92

Eliakim 132

Eliezer 10, 29

Eliezer, son of Moses 29

Elihu 188

Elijah xviii, 118, 119, 120, 121, 123, 124, 170

Elimelekh 189

Elisha 119, 121, 122, 123, 124

Elkanah 91

Elon 86

Enoch 4

Ephraim 17, 19, 85, 86, 89, 109, 161

Esau 10, 11, 13, 14, 59

Esther ix, 192

Euphrates 7, 53, 63, 73, 113, 153

Eve xi, 3

Evill-Merodach 133, 154

Ezekiel viii, 155

Ezra xii, xix, 200, 201, 203

Gabriel 199

Gad 12, 56, 57, 73, 79, 110

Galilee 127

Gath 93, 97, 99, 101, 110, 125

Gaza 78, 88

Gedaliah 152

Gehazi 122, 123

Gerar 8, 11

Gershom 22, 29

Geshur 108

Gezer 114

Gibeah 89, 95

Gibeon 77

Gihon 111

Gilboa 102

Gilead 85, 95, 127

Gilgal 75, 77, 94, 95

Golan 60

Goliath 97, 98, 99, 110

Gomorrah 8

Goshen 19, 25, 26

Greece 199

Habakkuk viii, 166

Hagar 7, 9

Haggai 167

HAGGAI 167

Haggith 111

Ham 5

Haman 193, 194

Hamath 57, 126, 128

Hanamel 149

Hananiah, Daniel's friend 196

Hananiah son of Azzur 149

Hannah 91

Hanun 106

Haran 5, 11, 12

Hazael 123, 124, 125

Hazor 78, 82, 83

Heber 83

Hebrew v, xv, xvi, xvii, xviii, xix, 11, 21, 22, 23, 30, 42, 64, 76, 150, 205, 207, 209

Hebrews 24, 96

Hebron 10, 14, 79, 82, 103, 104, 108

Heshbon 52

Hezekiah xi, 128, 129, 130, 131, 134, 138, 139, 165, 167

Hilkiah 144

Hinnom. See Valley of Hinnom 145

Hiram 104, 113, 114

Hittite 10, 11, 106

Hittites 78, 81

Hivvites 78

Hofni 91

Horeb 22, 29, 60, 114, 119

Hosea 161

Hoshea son of Elah 127, 128

Hulda 131

Hushai 108, 109

Ichabod 92

Iddo 168

Isaac xi, 9, 10, 11, 14

Isaiah xi, xviii, 128, 130, 134, 135, 136, 137, 138, 139, 140, 141, 142, 165, 209

Ish-Bosheth 103, 104

Ishmael 7, 9, 10, 152

Ishmaelites 16

Ishmael son of Nethaniah 152

Israel vii, xi, xvi, xvii, xviii, xix, xx, 13, 15, 19, 20, 21, 23, 26, 27, 28, 29, 32, 33, 34, 35, 36, 37, 38, 39, 40, 41, 42, 43, 44, 45, 46, 47, 48, 49, 50, 52, 53, 54, 56, 57, 58, 59, 60, 61, 62, 63, 65, 66, 67, 68, 69, 73, 74, 76, 77, 78, 80, 81, 82, 83, 84, 85, 86, 88, 89, 90, 92, 93, 94, 95, 96, 97, 98, 102, 103, 104, 105, 106, 108, 109, 110, 113, 114, 115, 116, 117, 118, 119, 120, 121, 122, 123, 124, 125, 126, 127, 128, 129, 134, 135, 136, 137, 138, 139, 140, 141, 142, 143, 144, 146, 147, 149, 150, 153, 156, 157, 158, 159, 160, 161, 162, 163, 164, 165, 166, 167, 169, 170, 174, 176, 177, 178, 179, 180, 181, 182, 183, 189, 199, 200, 203, 205

Israelites xi, xvi, xix, 21, 22, 23, 24, 25, 26, 27, 28, 29, 31, 33, 35, 37, 39, 40, 41, 42, 44, 45, 46, 47, 48, 49, 51, 52, 53, 54, 55, 56, 57, 59, 60, 61, 62, 63, 65, 66, 67, 75, 76, 77, 78, 81, 82, 84, 85, 92, 96, 100, 129, 137

Issachar 12

Ithamar 44

Ivzan 86

Jabesh 95

Jabin 82

Jacob ii, xi, 10, 11, 12, 13, 14, 15, 17, 18, 19, 80, 136, 138, 139

Jair 85

Japheth 5

Jebusite 79, 104

Jebusites 78, 79

Jechoniah xi, 148, 149

Jedidiah 107

Jehoahaz, king of Israel 124

Jehoahaz, king of Judea 132

Jehoiachin xi, 132, 133, 148, 149, 154, 200

Jehoiakim 132, 147, 148, 150, 153

Jehoram, king of Israel 121, 123

Jehoram, king of Judea 123

Jehoshaphat 120, 122, 123

Jehosheva 125

Jehu 124, 125

Jephthah 85, 86

Jeremiah vii, 144

Jericho 53, 69, 73, 75, 76

Jeroboam xi, 115, 116, 117, 124, 126, 127, 132, 161, 163

Jeroboam II 126, 161, 163

Jerubaal 84

Jerusalem xi, xii, xviii, 77, 79, 81, 104, 105, 106, 108, 109, 110, 112, 116, 117, 120, 124, 125, 126, 127, 128, 129, 130, 131, 132, 133, 134, 135, 136, 137, 138, 140, 141, 142, 143, 144, 145, 147, 148, 149, 150, 151, 153, 154, 155, 156, 157, 158, 163, 167, 168, 169, 170, 177, 180, 181, 190, 192, 196, 198, 199, 200, 201, 202, 203, 204, 205

Jesse 97, 136

Jethro 22, 29

Jewish ii, xv, xvi, 169, 189, 192, 193, 194

Jews xii, 193, 194, 195, 197, 200, 201,

202, 205

Jezebel 118, 119, 120, 124

Jezreel 84, 101, 124

Joab 103, 104, 106, 107, 108, 109, 110, 111, 112

Joash, king of Israel 125, 126

Joash, king of Judea 124

Job xix, 156, 187, 188

Johanan 152

Jonah 126, 164, 165

Jonathan 95, 96, 98, 99, 100, 102, 103, 106, 108

Jordan 53, 55, 56, 57, 58, 59, 60, 73, 74, 75, 78, 79, 80, 84, 85, 109, 121, 122

Joseph xi, 12, 15, 16, 17, 18, 19, 20, 21, 27, 80

Joshua xvii, 29, 48, 49, 56, 59, 68, 69, 73, 74, 75, 76, 77, 78, 79, 80, 81, 82, 167, 168, 169

Joshua the high priest 167, 168, 169

Josiah xi, 116, 131, 132, 144, 157, 167

Jotham 126, 127, 134, 165

Judah xi, xviii, xix, 12, 15, 18, 33, 44, 79, 81, 88, 89, 103, 110, 115, 116, 169

Judea vii, xi, xii, xviii, 113, 116, 117, 118, 122, 123, 124, 125, 126, 127, 128, 129, 131, 132, 133, 134, 135, 136, 137, 138, 140, 144, 145, 146, 147, 148, 149, 150, 151, 152, 153, 154, 156, 158, 159, 161, 163, 164, 165, 167, 168, 169, 170, 189, 190, 196, 200, 201, 202, 203, 205

Judean 117, 120, 122, 123, 124, 126, 127, 132, 133, 140, 149, 152, 153, 154, 156, 192, 196, 200

Judeans 88, 149, 152, 153, 200, 205

Kadesh 51, 52

Kedar 137

Kedesh 79

Keturah 10

Kingdom of Israel xviii, 116, 117, 119, 124, 135, 137, 138, 161

King's Road 51, 52

Kiriath-Yearim 93, 105

Kish 94

Korah 49, 50, 55

Laban 11, 12, 13

Laben 173

Lake Kinnereth 57

Leah 12, 14

Lebanon 63, 73, 78, 114, 169

Levi 14

Levite 44, 55, 57, 64, 79, 89, 116

Levites 44, 45, 46, 50, 51, 55, 58, 62, 79

Lot 5, 6

Malachi 170

Manasseh 17, 19, 55, 57, 58, 73, 79, 83, 130, 131

Manasseh, king 131

Manoah 86

Mattaniah 133

Medes 137

Media 192, 193

Mediterranean Sea 57, 63, 73

Menahem 127

Mephibosheth 106, 108
Merab 98
Merom 78
Mesha 122
Meshach 196
Methuselah 4
Micah 165
Michael 199
Michal 98, 101, 104, 105
Midian 10, 22, 23, 29, 47, 56, 83, 84
Midianite 53, 54, 55, 56, 84
Midianites 10, 54, 56, 83, 84
Miriam 28, 47, 48, 51, 67
Mishael 196
Mizpah 93, 95
Moab 8, 52, 53, 57, 59, 69, 82, 121, 122, 137, 145, 153, 158, 163, 189
Molekh 40, 132
Mordecai 192, 193, 194, 195
Moses xi, xvi, xvii, 21, 22, 23, 24, 25, 26, 27, 28, 29, 30, 31, 32, 33, 34, 35, 37, 38, 39, 40, 41, 42, 44, 45, 46, 47, 48, 49, 50, 51, 52, 54, 55, 56, 57, 58, 59, 60, 61, 62, 65, 67, 68, 69, 73, 75, 77, 79, 80, 114, 129, 170, 178
Moshe 22
Mount Ararat 4
Mount Carmel 119
Mount Ebal 68, 77
Mount Gerizim 68, 77
Mount Gilboa. See Gilboa 102

Mount Hor 52, 57
Mount Horeb. See Horeb 60
Mount Nebo 69
Mount of Olives 108, 170
Mount Sinai xvi, xvii, 29, 33, 35, 42, 43, 46
Mount Tabor 83
Naaman 122
Nabal 100
Nadab 33, 38, 44, 117
Nadab, son of Jeroboam 117
Nadav 33
Nahash 95, 106
Nahor 5, 10
Nahum 166
Naomi 189
Naphtali 12
Navoth 120
Nebo. See Mount Nebo
Nebuchadnezzar xi, xii, 132, 133, 148, 150, 152, 153, 154, 157, 158, 190, 192, 196, 197, 198, 199, 200, 205
Nebuzaradan 152, 154
Necho 132
Negev 6, 52
Nehemiah xii, xix, 202, 203, 204
Nile 21, 24
Nimrod 5
Nineveh 164, 165, 166
Noah xi, 4, 5, 156
Nov 99
Nubia 137, 158

Nubian 47, 151

Obadiah 164

Obed-Edom 105

Og 52, 56, 57, 59, 60, 85

Oholiav 33, 35

Omri 118

Ophir 114

Orpah 189

Othniel 81

Pashhur 147

Pekah 127, 135

Pekahiah 127

Peretz 16

Perizzites 78

Persia xii, 133, 140, 167, 192, 193, 195, 198, 199, 200, 201, 202, 203, 205

Persian 200

Persian Empire xii

Persians 198

Pethuel 162

Pharaoh 6, 16, 17, 18, 19, 21, 22, 23, 24, 25, 26, 27, 112, 114, 132, 151, 158

Philistia 137, 153, 158, 163, 169

Philistine 11, 78, 86, 87, 88, 89, 93, 95, 96, 98, 99, 101, 121

Philistines 8, 11, 78, 81, 82, 85, 86, 87, 88, 89, 92, 93, 94, 96, 97, 98, 99, 100, 101, 102, 105, 106, 110, 113, 123, 126, 129, 205

Phineas 54, 80

Phoenician 118

Pinchas 54

Pinehas 91, 92

Pithom 21

Potiphar 16

Poti-Phera 17

Promised Land xvii, xix, 5, 31, 42, 49, 50, 55, 57, 59, 62, 68, 69

Puah 21

Pul 127

Ra'amses 21

Rabbah 106, 107

Rachel 12, 14, 15, 17, 149

Rahab 73, 74

Ramah 99, 100

Ramoth 60

Rebekah 10, 11

Rehoboam xi, 115, 116, 117

Rephidim 29

Retzin 127, 128, 135

Reuben 12, 19, 56, 57, 73, 79

Re'uel 22

Riblah 57

Ruth xix, 189, 190

Samaria xviii, 118, 119, 122, 123, 124, 125, 126, 127, 128, 129, 136, 137, 138, 148, 157, 161, 163, 165

Samson xvii, 86, 87, 88, 89

Samuel ii, iv, v, xvii, 91, 92, 93, 94, 95, 96, 97, 99, 100, 102, 103, 176, 177, 193, 205, 209

Sanvallat 202, 203

Sarah 7, 8, 9, 10, 141

Sarai 5, 6, 7

Sargon xi
Satan 168, 187
Saul xvii, 94, 95, 96, 97, 98, 99, 100, 101, 102, 103, 104, 106, 108, 109, 110, 112, 174, 176, 181, 205
Sea of Reeds 27, 28
Se'ir 14
Sennacherib xi, 129, 130, 138, 139
Seth 3
Shadrach 196
Shallum 127
Shalmaneser xi, 128
Shamgar 82
Sheba, queen of 114
Sheba, rebel leader 110
Shechem 13, 14, 79, 80, 84
Shem 5
Shemaiah 116
Shifra 21
Shiloh 79, 91, 92, 115
Shim'i son of Gera 109, 112
Shishak 117
Shlomo 107
Shomron 118
Shushan 192, 193
Sidon 118
Sihon 52, 56, 57, 59, 60, 85
Simeon 12, 14, 17, 18, 19, 81
Sisra 82, 83
Sodom 6, 8
Solomon xi, 107, 111, 112, 113, 114, 115, 117, 177, 183, 189, 205

Susa 192
Talmai 108
Tamar 15, 107
Tamar, David's daughter 107
Tarshish 115, 165
Terah 5
Teresh 192
Tiglath-Pileser xi, 127, 128
Timnah 86
Tola son of Pua 85
Topheth 131, 145, 147
Tsiva 108
Tso'ar 8
Tyre 104, 113, 137, 158, 163
Ur 5
Uriah 106
Uriahu 148
Utz 187
Uzza 105
Uzziahu xi, 126, 127, 134, 135, 170
Valley of Hinnom 131, 145, 147
Vashti 192
Xerxes xii
Ya'akov 10
Yael 83
Yotham 84
Zadok 111
Zebulun 12
Zechariah, king, 126
Zechariah, prophet 169, 200
Zedekiah 133, 147, 148, 149, 150, 151, 152, 153, 154, 156, 157

Zelophehad 55, 58

Zephaniah 167

Zerah 16

Zeresh 193

Zerubbabel 167, 169, 200

Ziklag 102, 103

Zilpa 12

Zimri 118

Zion 114, 134, 136, 138, 139, 140,
    141, 142, 162, 163, 165, 166, 168,
    169, 176, 178, 179, 180, 181

Zipporah 22

www.ingramcontent.com/pod-product-compliance
Lightning Source LLC
Chambersburg PA
CBHW030227100526
44585CB00012BA/302